SnapShots 365!

Bible reading for
8- to 11-year-olds

First published 2012

ISBN 978 1 84427 738 4

Scripture Union
207–209 Queensway, Bletchley, Milton Keynes MK2 2EB, UK

This **Snapshots** material has appeared in previously published issues of **Snapshots**.

Writers: Sue Clutterham, Dave Godfrey, Gill Hollis, Judith Merell, Helen Parker, Paul Stockley, Doug Swanney, Janet Tilsley, Paul Wallis

Artist: Colin Smithson

Layout: Matt Evans, Coldfire Design Ltd

Cover design: kwgraphicdesign

Printed in India by Thomson Press India Ltd

Scripture Union is an international Christian charity working with churches in more than 130 countries.

Thank you for purchasing this book. Any profits from this book support SU in England and Wales to bring the good news of Jesus Christ to children, young people and families and to enable them to meet God through the Bible and prayer.

Find out more about our work and how you can get involved at:

www.scriptureunion.org.uk (England and Wales)

www.suscotland.org.uk (Scotland)

www.suni.co.uk (Northern Ireland)

www.scriptureunion.org (USA)

www.su.org.au (Australia)

Hi and welcome to...

Did you know that God's not only with you all the time, but he wants to talk with you and listen to you, too? Using **Snapshots** is a great way to help you understand what God is saying through his Word, the Bible.

Each day **Snapshots** gives you a few Bible verses to read, something to think about or do, and a prayer idea. If you can, find someone to read it with you. Find somewhere quiet, away from the TV.

Ask God to help you understand it before you start, then read the first part on the page.

Hear from God as you read the verses from the Bible, then read and act on the rest of the **Snapshots** bit. Spend a bit of time talking with God, using the ideas on the page and your own ideas.

Finding your way round the Bible

The Bible is in two parts called the Old Testament and the New Testament. Matthew is the first book in the New Testament – the second part of the Bible.

Matthew 1:21

Each book of the Bible is broken up into chapters. Matthew has 28 chapters and this verse is in the first chapter.

Matthew 1:21

Each chapter is split into verses, which are usually shown as very small numbers. This is verse 21.

Matthew 1:21

Use the Contents page in your Bible to find out where each book starts.

contents

No more

1 Jan

Happy New Year! Let's start the year with some really happy verses...

After he rose from the dead, Jesus went back to heaven to be with God. This week we'll get a bigger picture of what heaven will be like.

Read Revelation 21:1–4.

What will be there in heaven, the New Jerusalem?

____

What will not be there?

____

Take verse 4 and work out your own signs for each phrase. Now talk with God, using the signs, thanking him that heaven will be like that.

Brand new

2 Jan

God gave John several dreams or visions that we can read about in Revelation, the last book in the Bible. John was in prison on the island of Patmos when he wrote them down.

Read Revelation 21:5–7.

What is God, who is sitting on the throne, saying?

I will make everything clean/new/shining.

I am the beginning and the end/the middle/the cooling place.

I give refreshment and water sometimes/freely/a few drops at a time.

Everyone who is with me at the end will be my children/people/friends.

Thank God that in heaven nothing will be broken or dried up or dirty! It will be new!

He knows your name

3 Jan

How many names do you have? Include nicknames or ways that describe you such as "Mrs Smith's son".

Read Revelation 21:22–27.

Join the pictures to the questions:

What is heaven described like?

What shines on the city?

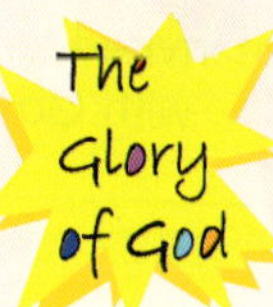

What will kings bring?

Read verse 27 again. Everyone who loves Jesus will have their name written in the Lamb's (Jesus') book of life and they will be in heaven. Imagine Jesus calling you by name. How does that make you feel?

Wish you were here

4 Jan

Do you like getting postcards from friends? When you go on holiday, do you send postcards? What do you write about?

Read Revelation 22:1–2.

Imagine you have just arrived in heaven. Write a postcard to one of your friends, telling them what it's like.

HEAVEN MAIL

Dear ________________

Well, here I am in heaven!

There is a ________________ flowing through the middle.

It's called the river that gives ________________.

It comes from the ________________ of God!

There is a __________ which gives __________.

The leaves are for ________________!

Read the verses again and then thank God that heaven is so amazing. (Psst! What picture of heaven would you want to put on the other side of the postcard?)

What will happen?

5 Jan

Before you go somewhere on holiday, you probably want to know what you can do when you get there. Maybe you ask if you can go swimming or mountain biking or...

Read Revelation 22:3–5.

Put a tick by the right answers and a cross by the wrong ones: [add tick box beside each]

In heaven, God's people will...

- ☐ worship God
- ☐ see God's face
- ☐ sit on a cloud and play a harp
- ☐ have God's name on their foreheads
- ☐ need a lamp
- ☐ have God as their light
- ☐ fly around with wings
- ☐ rule as kings for ever

Lord, we can't really imagine heaven, but we do know that it will be awesome. Best of all, we will be with you for ever and ever!

An invitation

6 Jan

Do you ever get invited to parties? Jesus has a special invitation for everyone, because he wants us to be in heaven with him. That will be some party!

Complete this invitation:

Invitation!

____
(your name)

is invited to celebrate in heaven with God, who offers you

____
(verse 17)

Please accept what God wants to give you. Come!

Read Revelation 22:16–17.

If you have already said "Yes", or want to say "Yes", to the invitation that Jesus gives, tell God about it now and talk to the person who gave you Snapshots.

If you haven't said "Yes" yet, keep thinking about it and ask that person to pray for you!

Special offer!

7 Jan

Can you get from GIFT to LOVE in five stages, changing only one letter at a time?

GIFT

_ _ _ _

_ _ _ _

_ _ _ _

LOVE

Jesus loved us so much that he died to save us from all the wrong things we do.

Now can you get from LOVE to SAVE in five stages, again only changing one letter at a time?

LOVE

_ _ N _

_ _ _ _

_ _ _ _

SAVE

(Answers on page 192.)

Escape!

8 Jan

The city of Nineveh was the capital of Assyria (a country in the Middle East). The Assyrians were enemies of Israel, God's special people.

Read Jonah 1:1–3.

What did God tell Jonah to do?

____

What did Jonah do instead?

____

What happens when someone asks you to do something you don't want to?

What if God asked you to do something you didn't want to do?

What would you think? What would you do?

Ask God to help you to be obedient to him.

Storm

9 Jan

Have you ever been to the beach? The sea looks lovely when the sun's shining... but in a storm it looks really fierce.

Imagine being on a boat in a storm...

Read Jonah 1:4–10.

How did the sailors feel about the storm?

What did Jonah feel about the storm?

What did Jonah say about God?

Use Codebreaker 1 on page 48 to find out:

UR / ZNQR / GUR / FRN

_ _ /_ _ _ _ / _ _ _ / _ _ _

NAQ / GUR / QEL / YNAQ

_ _ _ /_ _ _ / _ _ _ / _ _ _ _

Ask God to keep safe all people who work on the sea. Who can you think of?

Splash! Gulp!

10 Jan

Do you ever have an uncomfortable feeling inside when you've done something wrong? Jonah was feeling very uncomfortable on board ship...

Read Jonah 1:11–17.

Jonah thought the storm was all his fault, but who was really in control?

Fit these words correctly into the grid: FISH, JONAH, CALM, STORM, SEA, THROW, DROWN

The four letters in the yellow squares spell the answer.

Lord, you can do anything! You made the storm, you calmed the storm and you rescued Jonah.

You're amazing!

Rescue

11 Jan

Have you ever been really scared? Jonah was scared stiff! Try and imagine being inside the big fish.

Read Jonah 2:1–2,5–10.

What did Jonah do as soon as the fish swallowed him?

Find three things God did for Jonah (verses 2 and 6 will help).

1 ______________________

2 ______________________

3 ______________________

What did Jonah say he would do? (verse 9)

____

____

Think of a time when God has helped you. Write a thank you prayer inside the fish shape.

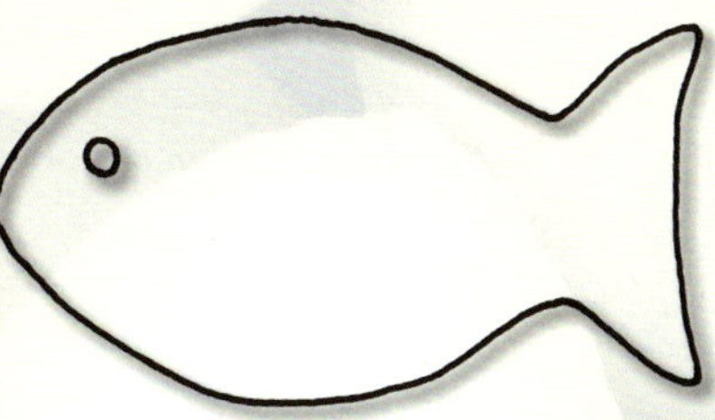

Sorry

12 Jan

When you've done something wrong, how do you show that you're sorry? Jonah obeyed God and went to Nineveh – but what would the Ninevite people do?

Read Jonah 3:1–10.

What did the people wear as a sign that they were sorry?

____

What did they need to do to prove they were sorry?

Stop ______________ and ______________

What did God do?

____

Sometimes it's easy to say sorry but not really mean it. The people of Nineveh said it and did it.

Dear Lord, I'm sorry for ______________.

Help me not to do ______________ again.

Thank you for forgiving me.

(Psst! Discover more about sackcloth on the next page.)

Sulking

13 Jan

Have you ever sulked about anything? You're not alone. Jonah sank into a mega-sulk!

Jonah 4:1–11.

Put numbers by the pictures to get the story in the right order.

Jonah sulked because God had forgiven the people of Nineveh! He forgot that God loves everyone, not just the people who have grown up loving him.

Use Jonah's words as a prayer: "You are a kind and merciful God, and you are very patient. You always show love, and you don't like to punish anyone."

Sackcloth

14 Jan

When Jonah told the people of Nineveh the things they had done wrong, they all started wearing sackcloth. So what is "sackcloth" and what was it used for? Sackcloth was a type of black cloth, made out of goats' hair.

Robes, belts, skirts and even clothes for animals were made out of it. It was worn next to the skin, so it must have been very itchy and uncomfortable – like an itchy woollen jumper that makes your skin go all funny – ugh!

People wore sackcloth:

- to show how they were feeling.
- to show they were sad when something bad had happened, like someone had died.
- to show they wanted to pray and talk to God.

The people of Nineveh wore sackcloth because they wanted to show how sorry they were for disobeying God.

New start

15 Jan

Have you done or tried anything new recently? New things were starting up for a young man called Timothy long ago...

Read Acts 16:1–5.

What did people think of Timothy (verse 2)?

- ☐ No one had a good word to say about him.
- ☐ Everyone spoke well of him.

What was Timothy's job (verse 4)?

- ☐ To go to the beach and relax.
- ☐ To tell followers of Jesus how to live by God's rules.

Thank God for the special job that Timothy did. Do you think God might have a special job for you, too? Talk to him about how that makes you feel.

Dream team

16 Jan

Can you remember any dreams you've had? In Bible times, God sometimes used dreams to tell people what to do.

Read Acts 16:6–12.

Can you draw Paul's dream or write what was said?

Father God, thank you for guiding Paul to do what you wanted him to do. Amen.

Here are the modern names of some countries Paul visited on his travels nearly two thousand years ago.

Italy Greece Cyprus
Turkey Sicily Malta

Have you been to any of them?

It's not fair

17 Jan

Have you ever helped someone and then got into trouble for it? Find out how that happened to Paul and his friend Silas.

Read Acts 16:16–24.

Cross out the wrong words:

Paul and his friends helped a woman/man. She was a slave and made lots of money/hamburgers for her owners.

When her owners realised they wouldn't be able to make any more sausages/money, they were really pleased/very cross. They took Paul and Silas to the beach/ Roman officials. They were beaten and thrown into a swimming pool/jail.

Was it easy for Paul and Silas to follow Jesus? Why do you think they didn't give up?

Please God, help me to keep on following you even when it's hard. Please help me especially when

____

Prisoners

18 Jan

The writer of today's Snapshot says, "Many years ago, my uncle was a missionary in Iran. He was put in prison because the government didn't want him to tell other people about Jesus. After he was released he told us that he used to sing hymns in prison!"

Read Acts 16:25–30.

As you read what happened to Paul and Silas in prison, do a "thumbs up" sign for good things that happened, and a "thumbs down" for bad things that happened.

What started as bad news became something that ended with good news. Why?

Thank God that his power can change things and make bad news into good news!

Even the jailer...

19 Jan

The thing about being a follower of Jesus is that you are never quite sure what will happen next! It was like that for Paul and Silas in prison...

Read Acts 16:31–35.

One minute the jailer was putting Paul and Silas' feet between heavy blocks of wood (verse 24), the next minute he was washing their wounds and giving them something to eat (verses 33–34)! God was working in an amazing way to rescue Paul and Silas! Why were the jailer and his family so happy (verse 34)?

Because they b________ i___ G_________

Please, God, help me to believe in you and the amazing things you can do, anywhere, any time.

Amen.

What happened next?

20 Jan

When Paul and Silas left prison they could have hurried away quickly, until they were as far away as possible. Is that what you would have done?

Read Acts 16:36–40.

Now read the last sentence twice because it's important!

Write down the first letter of each object below to find out what Paul and Silas did for the believers.

_ _ _ _ _ _ _ _ _

This means: "to give support, help or courage".

Thank you, God, that you helped Paul and Silas to encourage others, and not complain about being in prison.

Paul's travels

21 Jan

Paul, Silas and Timothy travelled a long way to tell others about Jesus. Many of the place names are different now.

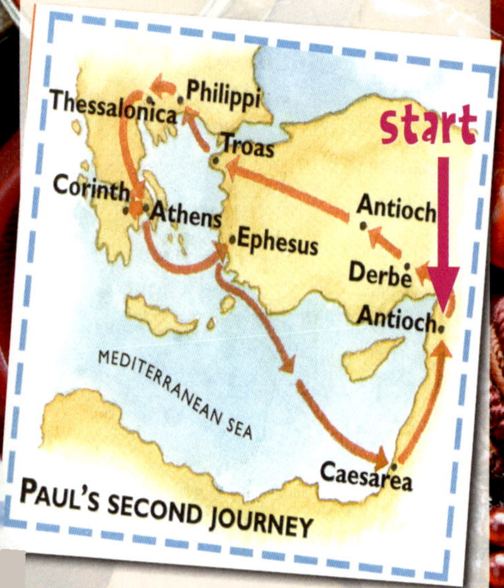

Get wise!

22 Jan

Proverbs are wise sayings. Being wise means to be clever and to know the right thing to do. There are lots of proverbs in the Bible.

Read Proverbs 1:1–6.

What are proverbs good for? Verses 3 and 4 tell us what they will help us to be like. Can you unscramble the words?

stoneh _ _ _ _ _ _ raif _ _ _ _

lervec _ _ _ _ _ _ _ or mrats _ _ _ _ _

Find the verse that says if you are already wise, the proverbs will make you wiser.

Father God, thank you that you give us your words in the Bible so that we can be smart and wise – the best that we can be.

Its a good look!

23 Jan

Do you have a cap that you look really cool in? Girls, what about a necklace that makes you feel pretty?

Read Proverbs 1:7–9.

Who's the first person we need to respect and obey?

____

Who else do we need to obey?

____

Obeying God and our parents is a good look! Draw a picture of yourself wearing a hat or necklace.

You don't hide a hat or necklace – anyone can see them. Do you let others see that you obey God and your parents instead of pleasing yourself?

Thank you, God, for people who give us good advice and for the advice you give us in the Bible.

The search

24 Jan

Being wise and listening to good advice is smart, but how do you get wise advice?

Read Proverbs 2:1–8.

Looking for wisdom is like searching for hidden treasure (verse 4). Can you find your way through the maze to reach it?

Use Codebreaker 1 on page 48 to fill in the blanks.

The hidden treasure is the JVFQBZ _ _ _ _ _ _ that comes from the YBEQ _ _ _ _

Think of the different ways we can discover the wisdom that comes from the Lord. Thank God for these!

Get it right!

25 Jan

Has anyone ever been mean or unkind to you? Have you ever wondered why they were like that? Look for it in this reading.

Read Proverbs 2:9–15.

It's not always clear what the results will be when we do things. God's wisdom helps us to know what is right and fair (verse 9). It will protect us from doing wrong (verse 12). Make a list of some of the bad things that you have seen or heard people do, then write the way that you think God would want them to be.

the wrong way	the right way

If we all obeyed God's wise words everything would be fair all the time.

Lord God, please help me to be enthusiastic about doing the right thing.

Too Smart

26 Jan

Imagine always knowing the right and best thing to do. Wouldn't it be great?

Read Proverbs 3:5–7.

Only God can show us the right way to live. Take out the Xs and Zs to see what we need to do to live the way God wants us to.

TxrzuxsztxtzhxezLxozrxd

When should we remember to trust God and let him lead us?

Azlzwxazyxsaznxdzixnz
exvzexrzyxtzhxiznxg

Which is your favourite part of today's Bible verses? Read them to someone else in your family and ask them their favourite bit.

See who can learn one of the verses first.

Being corrected

27 Jan

When you do a maths test and your teacher tells you that some of your answers are wrong, they do this because... (tick the right boxes)

- [ ] The teacher can't do maths.
- [ ] They want you to get better at maths.
- [ ] They like correcting you.

Read Proverbs 3:11–12.

The Lord corrects us for one reason alone, because he...

Fill in the crossword clues to find out.

1 The colour of the sky.
2 It sails on a river.
3 The opposite of under.
4 Helps keep your trousers up.
5 It shines in the sky.
6 You can play this on an instrument.
7 You swim in this at the beach.

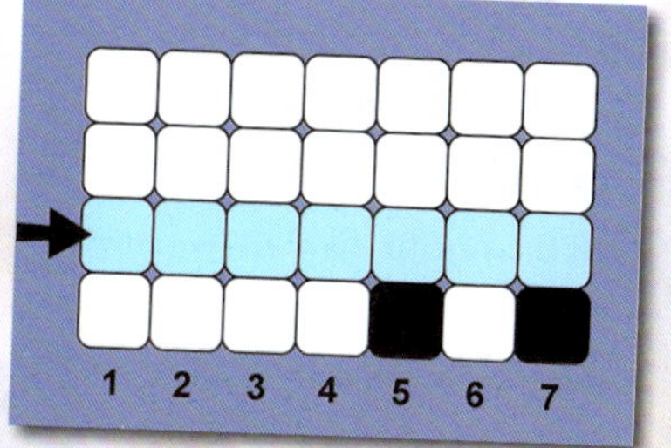

Dos and don'ts

28 Jan

Shut your eyes and imagine one of your friends or a neighbour you know.

Draw a picture of them, or write their name here:

Now read how God wants you to care for them.

Read Proverbs 3:27–30.

These verses are a list of 'dos and don'ts'.

How many 'dos' can you find? ☐

How many 'don'ts' are there? ☐

Now choose one of the 'dos or don'ts'. Look at your friend's picture, or their name, and ask God to help you treat them like that.

Be careful!

29 Jan

The last verses we read were mostly 'don'ts' and one 'do'. This time, the verses are mostly 'dos'...

Read Proverbs 4:20–27.

Which verse is about what we think?

Which verse is about what we say?

Which verse do you need to take most notice of now?

Ask God to help you remember the verse you chose, so that you can do what it says. Start by saying, "Please, God, help me to...", then read the verse.

Why not write the verse down on card and use it as a bookmark for your Bible?

Be like an ant!

30 Jan

Next time you go outside, look for an ant! Watch it carefully for a few minutes. See how busy it is – not just some of the time, but all the time!

Read Proverbs 6:6–11.

The word "ant" appears in this ant box seven times. See if you can find them all. (Ask a grown-up to explain any words you don't understand.)

Can you think of more "ant" words about the Bible verses?

Proverbs 6 says we can't be lazy. We should be like ants, otherwise we shan't get anything done. The Bible is adamant we should be anti-laziness and anticipate being busy

Don't be reluctant to work hard!

Ask God to help you be like an ant! (You might like to say in what way.)

Serious stuff!

31 Jan

If we want to live God's way, we have to take the Bible seriously – it's God's words written for us to read. It really is!

Read Proverbs 11:12–13 aloud.

What do you think God might be telling you in these verses?

Put a tick by the answers you think are correct.

- ☐ You can say whatever you like about someone if they can't hear you.
- ☐ It's better to keep quiet rather than gossip.
- ☐ Once you start gossiping, it's difficult to stop.
- ☐ It's OK to share another person's secret.
- ☐ Before you say something about someone, it's a good idea to ask yourself, "Is it true?", "Is it kind?" and "Is it helpful?"

Ask God to help you to follow the advice in verses 12 and 13.

Friends!

1 Feb

Sometimes at school people cause trouble and think they are being clever and funny. Do you know people like that?

Read Proverbs 24:1–2.

But if we shouldn't be friends with these people, how should we treat them? This is what Jesus said:

This is what I say to all who will listen to me:

"Love your enemies, and be good to everyone who hates you. Ask God to bless anyone who curses you, and pray for everyone who is cruel to you."

Luke 6:27–28 (CEV)

Please, God, help me to be wise when I am with my friends.

Be content!

2 Feb

If you were going to ask God for two things, what would they be?

Read Proverbs 30:7–9.

What two things did the writer ask God for?

1 ______________________________

____

2 ______________________________

____

What did he think would happen if he had too much? Tick the right box.

- ☐ He might eat too much.
- ☐ He might get a tummy ache.
- ☐ He might say he didn't need God.
- ☐ He might waste food.

What did he think would happen if he had too little? Unjumble the words.
eH higmt least

_ _ / _ _ _ _ _ / _ _ _ _ _

Thank God for the things you have. Ask him to help you be content with them.

☐

Evil Spirits

3 Feb

Evil spirits are real, but Jesus is more powerful than any evil spirit.

Ross Britza shares what happened in Malawi, Africa, just a few years ago:

An old lady came to see me. "My son is very sick. The doctor can do nothing for him." I drove to her village and five men were holding her son, who was screaming and shouting.

I knew in my heart that the young man was demon possessed. I said to the old lady, "There's something else we can try. We can pray for your son." Quietly I asked God to deliver this man and to give me faith to pray for him.

I looked at him and said, "Demon, in the name of Jesus I command you to leave this man at once!"

The man let out a sigh and lay back in his mother's arms peacefully. Later, he was fully recovered and playing with his two young children.

Praise God!

☐

Dear Timothy

4 Feb

Have you ever received a long, encouraging letter or email? Who was it from? What was it about?

Read 2 Timothy 1:1–5.

This Bible book is a letter from

_ _ _ _ to _ _ _ _ _ _ _ _.

Paul wasn't really Timothy's dad, but he had taught and encouraged Timothy as a good father would. Who else encouraged Timothy in his faith?

L _ _ _, his grandmother.

E _ _ _ _ _, his mother.

Lord, thank you for people who have encouraged my faith, especially

________________________.

Could you write a letter or email to encourage someone? Tell them it cheers you up when you think about them.

Don't be shy!

5 Feb

Timothy was a bit shy and timid. But that shyness didn't come from God. And God had given him something to overcome it.

Read 2 Timothy 1:6–8.

When we give God's Spirit room in our life, the Spirit gradually pushes out other things that stop us living for Jesus.

What does God's Spirit fill us with?

P _ _ _ _

L _ _ _

S _ _ _ - c _ _ _ _ _ _ _

Lord God, thank you for your Spirit in my life. Please help me to live in the power of your Spirit.

Grace

6 Feb

Do you know anyone called Grace? That name means “kindness you don’t deserve”.

Read 2 Timothy 1:9–10.

Why did God save us? Cross out the wrong answer.

God saved us...

because of what we have done.

because of his grace, his kindness.

Match up words which mean the same:

immortal	plan
purpose	everlasting
gospel	undeserved kindness
saviour	good news about Jesus
grace	rescuer

Have you ever heard anyone say you will go to heaven if you’re good? Is it true?

Lord God, thank you for sending Jesus to make me one of your people, even though I don’t deserve it.

Hold on

7 Feb

Have you ever played tug-of-war? What happens if you let go of the rope when the ‘war’ is still going on?

Read 2 Timothy 1:13–14.

What did Paul tell Timothy to hold on to or follow (verse 13)?

Draw a “rope” around the lines that you plan to hold on to. Draw them to the edge of the page.

God loves you.

God doesn’t care.

Jesus died for you.

Jesus isn’t real.

The Holy Spirit lives in you.

The Bible isn’t true.

Put your fingers on the “ropes” you have drawn and ask God to help you hold on to the truth about him.

Pass it on

8 Feb

Imagine passing the baton in a relay race. Careful! Don't drop it. Make sure the next person has it firmly.

Read 2 Timothy 2:1–2.

How was the gospel passed on? Fill in the names. You are one of the others. Add your name. Who could you pass the gospel message on to? Fill in their name in the last box.

paul t _ _ _ _ _ _

reliable p _ _ _ _ _ o _ _ _ _ _

Lord, help me to share my faith with __________. Help them to understand.

Prize winners

9 Feb

If you want to do really well at sport or music you probably have to 'suffer' a bit. Like practising when you'd rather be doing something else. You have to think of the future.

Read 2 Timothy 2:3–7.

What are these people working at? Write in the spaces.

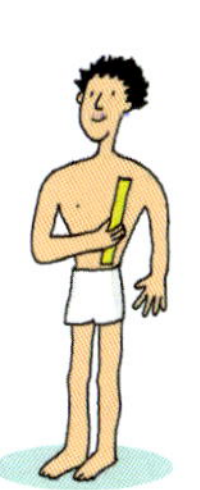

Who or what can we focus on when it's hard to live the Christian life?

Lord, help me to focus on pleasing you and think of heaven, especially when things are difficult.

Think ahead

10 Feb

Have you ever made a complicated model, done a sponsored swim or walk or learned to play a musical instrument? How long did it take?

Read 2 Timothy 2:22–25.

It takes a long time to develop a good character.

Paul told Timothy to aim for faith, love, peace and a pure heart, and to be good, patient, gentle and kind. Find these words in the wordsearch.

T	A	P	G	E	R	K	S	O
N	N	A	O	L	G	I	I	T
E	P	L	P	V	E	N	Y	M
I	O	E	D		N	D	R	E
T	L	F	A	I	R	H	I	K
A	E	J	E	C	L	S	U	S
P	U	R	E	H	E	A	R	T

Write out the leftover letters from the wordsearch and make them into a prayer.

Help me to have

_ / _ _ _ _ _ _ _ _ _ _ _ _ /

_ _ _ _ / _ _ _ _ / _ _ _ _ _

Powerful words!

11 Feb

If your favourite teacher was leaving, what final instructions would they give you?

Read 2 Timothy 3:14–17.

The lines of this chant are mixed up. Sort it out and write the line numbers in the box below.

1 But now you're tall

2 They wisely gave you

3 Your teachers all taught you the Scriptures

4 As for you

5 Keep your view fixed on the Scriptures

6 So every day try to read the Scriptures

7 You were small

8 You know what's true

9 The truth to save you

4		
	1	
		6

Tap a rhythm as you chant it. (Go to page 192 for the answer.)

Lord, help me to keep reading your Scriptures and to learn from them to live your way.

what's it good for?

12 Feb

Would you like to be fully qualified? You've got what you need inside the covers of your Bible!

Read 2 Timothy 3:16–17.

Tick what these verses say the Bible does for us:

- ☐ Teaches maths.
- ☐ Corrects faults.
- ☐ Tells us how to live right.
- ☐ Teaches truth.
- ☐ Gives us friends.
- ☐ Tells us about Noah.
- ☐ Points out wrong beliefs.

On paper, draw yourself (with a Bible in your hand) fully equipped to serve God. What are you ready for? Unscramble the letters.

Yerve ndik fo odog edde

_ _ _ _ _ / _ _ _ _ _ / _ _ /

_ _ _ _ / _ _ _ _

Ask God to show you a good deed you can do for him.

Tell others

13 Feb

Do you think teaching is an easy job?

Do you know a teacher who can... convince, encourage, tell you off, be patient, keep their temper, give correct information, put up with difficulties and perform their whole duty? Paul told Timothy to do all of that!

Read 2 Timothy 4:1–5.

Paul begins very seriously because his message is so important. Take out the Qs and Zs to find out what Paul predicts.

Pqeqzozpqle wzizlzl nqoqt lqizsqtzeqn tzo gqozoqd tzeqazcqhziqnzg sqoquznqd dqozcqtzrqiznqe. Tqhzeqy wqizlzl tquqrzn aqwzazy fqrzozm lzizsztzeqnziznqg tqo tzhqe tqrquztzh.

But what did Paul tell Timonthy to keep doing (verse 5)?

Thank God for good teachers who have taught you at school or who have told you about God.

Do your best

14 Feb

What do you find difficult to stick at? Write it in the running track, then talk to God about it.

Read 2 Timothy 4:6–7.

Did Paul say he won the race? YES/NO

What did he claim (verse 6)?

I have ____________________

I have run the _______________

I have ____________________

Now he is ready to __________

____

But he isn't sad or afraid. Find out why tomorrow!

The great prize

15 Feb

Have you ever won a prize? What was it? What did you do to win it?

Read 2 Timothy 4:8.

Paul knew he would be welcome in heaven because he would be EVTUG JVGU TBQ.

Use Codebreaker 1 on page 48 to crack the code and write it in the trophy.

Paul said the prize was not only for him and Timothy, but for all who love God. Write your name and the names of other Christians you know on the winners' plaques.

Lord, help me to serve you energetically all my life, so that at the end of my life I'll look forward to receiving my prize from you.

Prayer time

16 Feb

Do you have a person or a situation you want to keep praying for? Don't trust your memory. Find a trigger and use it!

Not the sort of trigger that's on a gun! A trigger is just something that makes something else happen. When you sit in a chair with the TV remote, the remote is a trigger that can make the TV change channels.

A light switch is a sort of trigger too. It makes the light go on and off. So here's the big question: what triggers could get you to pray?

Here's what some people said:

TANIA: When I get asthma and I cough a lot, I let it remind me to pray for people I know who are new Christians.

JAN: I keep a smooth stone in my pocket, and whenever I put my hand in my pocket and feel it, I pray for my son.

A house for God

17 Feb

Imagine if you could create your perfect dream house! Think what you would build. Now think bigger! Think about a palace fit for a king or queen.

Now think even bigger! Think of a perfect house big enough for God!

Read 2 Chronicles 2:1–4.

How many people were to help Solomon with his big plans? (If you can't work it out the answer is in verse 17.)

The Temple was a special house where people met with God. Where can you meet with God? At church? In the park? In your house?

Walk around your house. Draw a plan (or build a model!). Thank God that you can meet him everywhere.

Skills and creativity

18 Feb

Do you enjoy working with your hands? What are you good at making? Different people have different abilities. Solomon chose skilled craft workers to help build the Temple.

Read 2 Chronicles 2:5–7 and 2:11–13.

Make a list of all the things to be used in building the Temple. What sort of workers do you think were needed? (Cross out the wrong answers.)

People who could... cut stone, unblock drains, weave cloth, carve wood, fix electrics, stitch fabrics, weld metal, bend plastics.

Creativity is a gift from God. Say thank you to God for all the skills and abilities you have.

Think: How can you use your abilities for God?

Big and beautiful!

19 Feb

How big is your house? Try to measure it. How many paces long and wide is it? What are the main colours? And what is the doorway like? Describe it out loud.

Read 2 Chronicles 3:3–9.

Try to imagine what the Temple must have been like.

Find a tape measure, then start measuring out the size of the holiest room in the Temple (see verse 8).

You'll probably have to stop before you get to the end! Now imagine the walls covered in gold. Not just gold paint, but pure solid gold! Awesome!

God doesn't live in a temple. God lives in you. You are more valuable than all the gold in the Temple. Think about that.

Flights of fantasy

20 Feb

Do you ever read superhero comics? They are full of fantastic creatures that do amazing things. Comic book artists love to let their imaginations run wild.

God gave the Temple craft workers good imaginations too!

Read 2 Chronicles 3:10–14.

What did they have to make?

They also had to weave a cloth curtain using bright colours.

Untangle the threads to work out the colours:

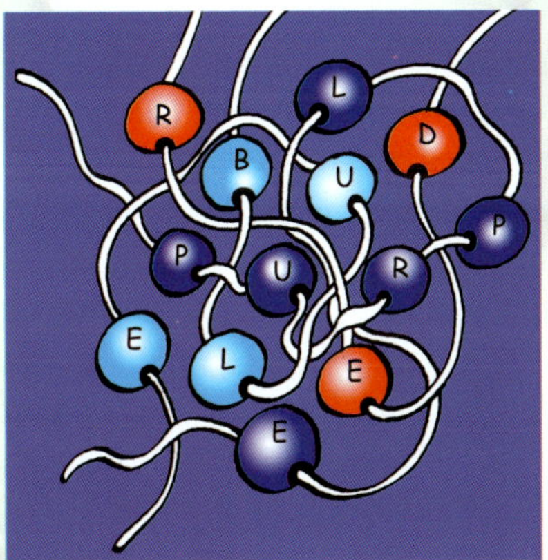

(Psst! These colours were the most expensive dyes.)

Thank God for your mind and imagination!

Dedicated to God

21 Feb

In the Temple there were lots of elaborate items used by the priests when they led worship.

Read 2 Chronicles 4:1 and 4:19 – 5:1.

All of these items were dedicated to God and not used for anything else.

You can be dedicated to God too.

Dedicate your hands (will you use them in kind ways?).

Dedicate your mouth (will you speak words of encouragement?).

Dedicate your eyes (will you see God's world?).

Dedicate your mind (will you think clean thoughts?).

Thank God for all the special things dedicated for worship in the Temple. Ask God to make you dedicated to him.

Sacred memory

22 Feb

Do you have a place where you keep special things? The people kept the covenant box (or sacred chest) in the Temple. It was a sign of God's promise, and a reminder of the solemn agreement made long ago by Moses.

Read 2 Chronicles 5:2–10.

What was kept inside the covenant box? (Unjumble the words.)

wot notes blatest

_ _ _ / _ _ _ _ _ _ / _ _ _ _ _ _ _ _

How do you remember God's promises to you?

Make a covenant book, with a page for each thing you learn about God. Keep it in a box and decorate it with other special things that remind you how wonderful God is!

God's radiance!

23 Feb

What is the brightest thing you have ever seen? When something is too bright we have to shield our eyes or look away, because it hurts to look at it.

Read 2 Chronicles 5:11–14.

How does God appear? Read every other letter to give two answers!

dsahziznliinnggclliioguhdt

_ _ _ _ _ _ _ _ _ / _ _ _ _ _ and

_ _ _ _ _ _ _ _ / _ _ _ _ _

Find a piece of bright yellow card. Cut out a dazzling cloud shape. Write on it: "God is brighter than the brightest light, shining in all glory." Stick it up next to your light switch or window.

Shut your eyes and imagine God's glory, pure and clean and radiant! Tell God how incredible and amazing he is.

Gods choice

24 Feb

If you had to pick one person from everyone you know, who would you choose to be with?

Read 2 Chronicles 6:1–6.

Use Codebreaker 1 on page 48 to decode the answers.

Where is the place God chose to meet the people?

WREHFNYRZ ____________________

Who is the person God chose to lead the people?

QNIVQ____________________

The people of Israel often rebelled, but God still chose to be with them. He was with them when they worshipped at the new Temple that Solomon built.

Thank God that he chooses to be with us too.

Kept or broken?

25 Feb

Answer these two questions:

How often do you keep your promises? (Circle one.)

Always, mostly, sometimes, never.

How often do friends keep their promises to you? (Circle one.)

Always, mostly, sometimes, never.

Do you know anyone who always keeps a promise?

Read 2 Chronicles 6:12–17.

What does God keep? What does God show? (Hint: see verse 14.) Solomon gives thanks because all God's promises come true. Not one of God's promises is ever broken.

Kneel down (just like Solomon) and think of some of God's wonderful promises. Now stand up and hold your hands up high (like Solomon did) and say: "Lord God, you always keep your promises. Thank you!" Ask God to help you keep your promises too.

Great forgiveness

26 Feb

Two new questions:

How often do you forgive your friends? (Circle one.)

Always, mostly, sometimes, never.

How often do your friends forgive you? (Circle one.)

Always, mostly, sometimes, never.

Read 2 Chronicles 6:18–21.

Solomon recognises that God is too great to live in a temple, even the beautiful one he has just built. Solomon humbly asks God to forgive the people when they do wrong. The amazing news is that God does forgive!

Are there things you need to say sorry to God for? God promises to forgive, so talk to God and put things right as soon as you can.

Ask God to help you forgive others too.

Ask for a blessing!

27 Feb

Are you a generous person? Do you enjoy giving things to others? God loves to give generously to people.

Read 2 Chronicles 6:40–42.

What does Solomon ask God? (Cross out the wrong words.)

Do not accept/reject your chosen king.

Stay out/here/away for ever.

Ignore/listen to the prayers.

Make the people sad/happy.

Celebrate because of your goodness/what you have done.

What do you want to ask God for? God delights to do what is good.

Ask God for two blessings: one for you and one for someone else.

God's come to stay!

28 Feb

Have you still got that cloud stuck on the wall by your light switch? (See page 32.) In today's story, the incredible bright light of God's glory is here again.

Everyone is overcome. They all fall face down in worship and adoration.

Read 2 Chronicles 7:1–6.

It must have been the most incredible experience! A clear sign of God's presence, beyond their wildest imagination.

This absolutely awesome God is with you every day! Imagine that!

Tell God how amazing and incredible he is. What words can you find to say how great and awesome God is?

Make up a new word to describe God!

A true story

29 Feb

Kel was only 8 when he woke up one night to hear his mum and dad shouting at each other in the next room. He couldn't believe it.

He'd never heard them yelling like that before. He was scared. What if his family broke up? He felt that his world was falling apart.

Kel felt so alone. He needed God to tell him that everything would be OK. Quietly he put the light on. No one noticed; the shouting continued. Kel picked up his Bible.

He wanted God to speak to him and he knew the Bible was God's Word so he started reading. Before long he found these words: Love never fails.

It was as if God was saying those words just to him. He could feel God in his spirit, telling him that he'd always love him. It was then he knew that no matter how bad things became, with God he'd somehow be OK.

Send for help

1 Mar

If we're unwell we go to the doctor, or if we are seriously ill he might pay us a visit at home. Life was different in Bible times.

Read John 11:1–6.

Now complete this crossword.

1 Who was sick?
2 Where did he live?
3 The name of his sister with the perfume.
4 The name of his other sister.
5 Who did they send for?

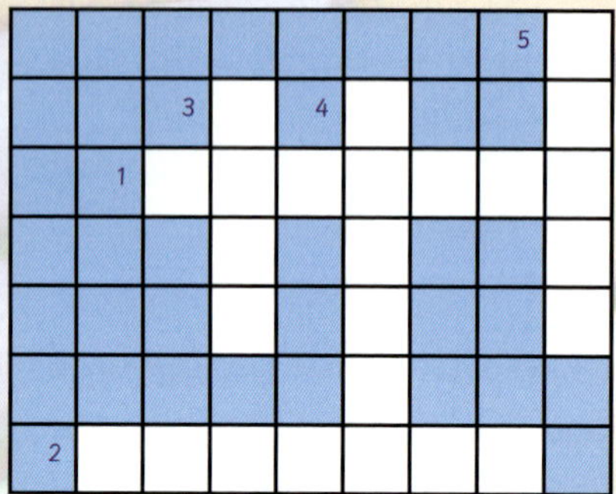

The sisters sent a message to Jesus. We can do the same. Pray for anyone you know who is unwell, and for the doctors and nurses looking after them.

Dead

2 Mar

Martha and Mary sent for Jesus because their brother was ill, but he did not go to them immediately. Jesus loved his friend Lazarus, but he had a better plan.

Read John 11:11–15.

Why is Jesus glad that he was not with Lazarus earlier, when he could have healed him from his illness?

Use Codebreaker 1 on page 48 to work out the answer.

ABJ LBH JVYY UNIR N
PUNAPR GB CHG LBHE
SNVGU VA ZR

_ _ _ / _ _ _ / _ _ _ _ / _ _ _ _
_ / _ _ _ _ _ _ / _ _ / _ _ _ /
_ _ _ _ / _ _ _ _ _ / _ _ / _ _

Lord, please help us when sad things happen. Help us to understand that you have a special plan for our lives and that you can help us to cope when we feel down.

Too late?

3 Mar

Have you ever been late for school, a party, church, handing in your homework?

Read John 11:17–23.

Martha assumes that things would have been different if Jesus had been there earlier...

Fill in the blanks from verse 21.

"If _____ had _____ here, _____,

my _____ would _____ have

_____!"

Flashback! Read John 11:4 again.

Jesus is never too late for anything. It is part of God's special plan that Lazarus has died. Thank you, God, that you have a special plan for my life. Thank you that you are with me whether I am late, early or on time.

Thank you that your timing is always perfect.

Next stop, heaven!

4 Mar

Can you think of anything Jesus said about himself? What he was about to tell Martha was the most amazing thing of all...

Read John 11:24–27.

What does Martha believe will happen to Lazarus?

What does Jesus say about himself?

What does Martha say about herself?

Colour in the dotted shapes to reveal the answer.

Thank you, Lord, that you have promised eternal life with you in heaven to everyone who believes in you. Help me to get excited about this now.

Tears of love

5 Mar

Do you do any of these things? Circle all the words that apply to you.

laugh	cry	smile
eat	hiccup	love
yawn	drink	talk
sneeze	blink	breathe

Did you circle all the words above? Which of these things does Jesus do in today's reading?

Read John 11:32–36.

How many words can you find in these verses that describe Jesus' feelings? Jesus would have done the same because, although he is God's Son, he was also completely human.

Lord, thank you that you always know exactly how I'm feeling because you have felt those things too.

Not impossible for God!

6 Mar

Check out the story so far! Lazarus is ill, his sisters send a message to Jesus, but by the time he gets there Lazarus is already dead. What happens next?

Read John 11:38–44.

Can you complete this triangle puzzle?

1 The man who is buried.

2 One of his sisters.

3 Jesus wanted everyone to believe and see God's _ _ _ _ _ _ .

4 The tomb was a _ _ _ _ .

5 Jesus said, "Lazarus, come _ _ _!"

6 and, "Untie him and let him _ _."

7 The number of days he was in the tomb.

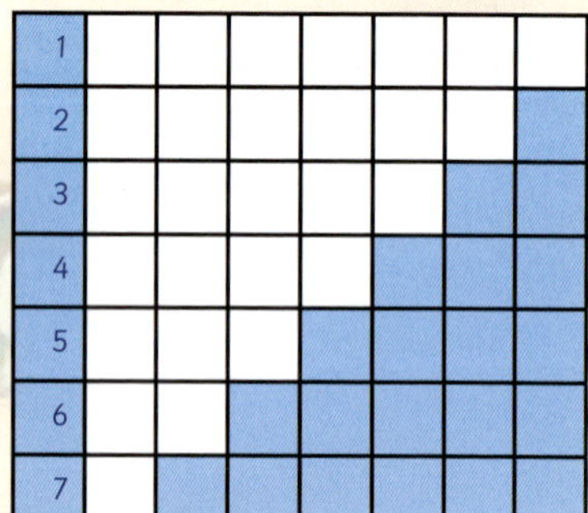

A special son

7 Mar

Have you ever sat next to someone naughty at school, or had a next-door neighbour who was a troublemaker?

The Philistines were troublemakers and they lived in the country next-door to the Israelites.

Read Judges 13:1–5.

What was the baby's special job (verse 5)?

____

Cross out the things Manoah shouldn't do.

Things to do

Have wine to celebrate
Bath the baby
Cut the baby's hair
Make toys for the baby

These things showed that the baby would be dedicated to God. Think of one action you do differently because you love God.

Ask God to help you to do this action today.

Samson the strong

8 Mar

Here's a riddle: Why is a policeman very strong?

(The answer is at the bottom of the page.)

Here's another question: Why was Samson so strong?

Read Judges 14:5–6.

It was God who helped Samson kill the lion. God gives many different gifts to people. Can you find these gifts in the wordsearch?

music	making friends
strength	reading
healing	kindness
helping	teaching

X	M	T	H	F	X	G	K
G	U	E	E	R	G	N	I
N	S	A	A	I	N	I	N
I	I	C	L	E	I	K	D
P	C	H	I	N	D	A	N
L	X	I	N	D	A	M	E
E	X	N	G	S	E	X	S
H	T	G	N	E	R	T	S

Because he holds up the traffic with one hand!

God helps Samson

9 Mar

Do you talk to your family when you come home from school? Wouldn't it be strange if you only talked to them on special occasions?

Read Judges 15:14–20.

Which of these would make the best newspaper headline?

SAMSON KILLS 1,000 PHILISTINES!

SAMSON DRINKS WATER FROM A ROCK!

But which event was the most important? Samson couldn't have done either of these things without God's help. God doesn't just help us when we do special things. He cares about us all the time.

Think of the most normal, boring, simple thing you will be doing this week... and ask God to help you with it.

Love is

10 Mar

Think about the people who care about you. How do they show their love to you?

Read Judges 16:4–9.

Do you think Samson trusted Delilah? Y/N

Do you think he should have been honest? Y/N

Do you think Delilah loved Samson? Y/N

In the heart, write down some words about true love.

1 Corinthians 13:4–8 will help you.

Father God, thank you that you love me. Please help me to love other people too. Amen.

A hair-raising story

11 Mar

Delilah didn't give up. She kept asking Samson the secret of his strength. Can you keep a secret? Samson couldn't...

Read Judges 16:15–22.

Why did Samson have long hair?

a) He didn't have any scissors. ☐

b) To show that he belonged to God. ☐

c) It was fashionable. ☐

Why did Delilah cut Samson's hair?

a) The Philistines paid her. ☐

b) She needed it for a false beard. ☐

c) To save money on shampoo. ☐

What happened when Samson lost his hair?

a) His head got cold. ☐

b) His muscles went flabby. ☐

c) God stopped helping him. ☐

In prison, Samson was still strong enough to turn a millstone to grind grain. So why wasn't he strong enough to beat the Philistines?

The Temple tumbles

12 Mar

When Jesus knew he had to die, he was really scared. He asked God to rescue him but said he was willing to do whatever God wanted.

What did Samson have to do that he thought he couldn't?

Read Judges 16:26–31.

Number these stones in the right order to read the message.

one ☐ Lord ☐ strong ☐
remember ☐
time ☐ last ☐ me ☐
prayed ☐ God ☐ Samson ☐
make ☐ please ☐ me ☐

Can you make up a pretend website address? If www stands for "when we're weak", fill in the rest.

For example www.Godwillhelpus.ok means "When we're weak God will help us, OK!"

www.____________________

Brotherly love

13 Mar

A boy called Harvey told **Snapshots**:

"Most of the time my brother, Matthew, and I get on well together. I know I should like him all the time, but when he's being annoying it's really difficult to like him.

One day we had a really big argument. Later that day we were playing in the park, but ignoring each other. A group of much bigger boys came into the park and ordered me off the swing.

I was a little bit frightened. Matthew saw what was going on so he walked over to the swings and told the boys to wait their turn. They said something back to him but went away.

Matthew really stood up for me, yet only five minutes earlier we'd been horrible to each other. It made me realise that even when we are cross with each other, we still love each other."

Being and doing

14 Mar

Can you think of some famous people? Are they sports stars, film stars, pop stars or world leaders? Are they famous because of what they do?

Read Psalm 8:1–2.

God is great, not only because of the amazing things he does, but because of who he is.

Can you match the right answers with these questions?

Where is his greatness seen?

Children and babies

Where does his praise reach?

All enemies

Who sings his praises?

In all the world

Who is he safe from?

To the heavens

Read Psalm 8:1–2 as a prayer, then add words of your own to praise God for his greatness.

Awesome

15 Mar

Can you look out of a window and see the sky? Think how big it is. How does it make you feel? Tell God now.

First read Genesis 1:16–18, then read Psalm 8:3–4.

How would you describe the moon and the stars to someone who couldn't see them?

There are more stars in the universe than there are grains of sand on all the beaches on the earth. Awesome! Turn over the page for stunning stats about the universe to amaze your friends.

Lord God, the universe is so great. There are millions of stars but I'm so small and there's only one of me. Thanks for knowing me and watching me and loving me.

What about us?

16 Mar

Today we're going to find out what our great, awesome Creator God thinks about us! Look out for surprises.

Read Psalm 8:5–9.

Draw yourself in the space below, then match the shapes together to find the missing words:

all creation important greatness world everything

God made us the next most ________________ to himself.

He made us to rule over ________________

He put us in charge of ________________

God's ________________ is seen in all the ________________

Read verse 9 of Psalm 8 as a prayer of praise to God.

Stunning stats

17 Mar

No one knows how big the universe is. Some scientists say it's getting bigger all the time; others think it's getting smaller. On a very clear night in the countryside you can see about 2,000 stars, but that's only a fraction of the stars out there.

The sun is our nearest star. It's 333,400 times bigger than earth. One million earths could fit inside the sun. The sun's temperature is 11,000 degrees Fahrenheit at the surface and 27 million degrees Fahrenheit at the centre. Stars can be all sorts of colours according to their temperature. Blue stars are very hot and red stars are cool. Our sun is yellow, which means it has a medium temperature.

Giant stars are 1,000 times brighter than the sun and are up to 200 times as wide. The largest stars are called Supergiants. The biggest ever found is 10 million times brighter than the sun.

What else can you discover about God's amazing universe?

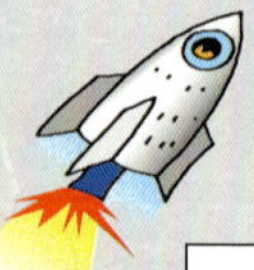

Friend into traitor

18 Mar

Jesus had done nothing wrong. He simply showed people what it was like to have God as their friend. But the religious leaders felt this was a threat to their power. They wanted to kill him. Judas, who had once been a friend of Jesus, decided to help them out.

Read Luke 22:1–6.

What sort of a person do you think Judas was?

Sometimes people are hated by others because of their religious beliefs. Can we disagree with others and still be friends?

How can you be a friend to others who are different from you?

In some places around the world Christians are hated for saying they have God as their friend. Ask God to help them to go on showing love to others.

Saying goodbye

19 Mar

It is hard to say goodbye to friends, knowing you might never see them again.

Read Luke 22:14–22.

What does Jesus give to his friends to help them never forget him?

What is Jesus telling his friends? (Circle all the right answers.)

He is going to have a party.

He is going to be killed.

God doesn't care.

It is part of God's plan.

He will not forget them.

Someone will betray him.

Remember me.

It is getting late.

Take a piece of bread and imagine Jesus telling his friends that his body is going to be broken. Say thank you that he was willing to follow God's plan.

Tough choices!

20 Mar

Sometimes you know you are going into a difficult or risky situation. But you have to face it, and do what you know is right.

Read Luke 22:39–46.

(Cross out the wrong words and fill in the gaps.)

Jesus **never/usually/sometimes** came here to pray.

He knew his task was **easy/clever/painful.**

What did Jesus pray?

God sent ______________________ to help him.

Jesus must have felt very lonely.

Do you know someone who is all alone and facing something really hard? What can you do to help them not feel so alone? Pray for them now.

Trusting God

21 Mar

Even when his life was threatened, Jesus did not use violence. He trusted God to be with him.

Read Luke 22:47–53.

Sort out the jigsaw pieces. Cross out the ones that are not God's way, circle the ones that are God's way of doing things.

Jesus even showed kindness to his enemies (see verse 51). How could you show kindness to someone who doesn't like you?

Help me, God, to learn to do things your way.

Let down

22 Mar

Have you ever been let down by a friend? How does it feel? Have you ever let someone down?

Read Luke 22:54–62.

Peter knew he had let Jesus down. How did he feel?

How do you think Jesus felt when he looked at Peter?

Some days later Jesus met Peter (see John 21:15–19) and let him know he was forgiven.

Do you think you have done something that is too bad for God to forgive? What does today's story say to you?

Find a handkerchief and hold it as you think about Peter's tears. Now ask God to forgive you for any bad things you have done.

Who is Jesus?

23 Mar

Every king has a government or an army! So what kind of a king is Jesus?

Read Luke 23:1–4.

Three accusations! Two are false, only one is true! Which one? Jesus is accused of...

misleading the people
telling people not to pay tax
saying he is a king

(Psst! The word "Messiah" means a special king anointed with the power of God's Spirit.)

Jesus was not a ruler like the emperor was, because God's kingdom is not like the Roman Empire!

Make a list of the differences between Pilate's empire and Jesus' kingdom.

(Psst! Pilate was the Roman Procurator in charge of Judea.)

Dear God, thank you that Jesus is a special king, who shows us your way of doing things.

Crowd turns nasty

24 Mar

In today's story we are in a court of law. Jesus is on trial and Pilate is the judge. Was his verdict GUILTY or NOT GUILTY? Read the passage then circle the right answer.

Read Luke 23:13–19.

Do you think everyone in the crowd meant what they said? If they really knew Jesus, would they want to kill him?

Decide now to choose some good friends (make a list), and not to join in with a bad crowd that will lead you astray.

Good friends

Dear God, I'm sorry for the times when I go along with a bad crowd, knowing it is wrong. Give me courage to do and say what is right.

Codebreaker 1

Codebreaker 2

a	b	c	d	e	f	g	h	i	j	k	l	m
!	"	£	$	%	^	&	*	(	)	-	+	=

n	o	p	q	r	s	t	u	v	w	x	y	z
[	]	{	}	@	#	~	<	>	?	/	_	'

Pilate against the people

25 Mar

Have you ever been punished for something you didn't do? Perhaps someone in authority (a leader or teacher) was supposed to stand up for you, but didn't.

Read Luke 23:20–25.

Did Pilate do his job well, or did he fail?

Link each choice to either PILATE or the CROWD. Which choice is left over? (The answer is on page 192.)

Pilate **Crowd**

pushy
weak
gave in
knew what was right
loud
strong
strong
did right

Find an old newspaper and cut out some pictures of people in authority. Stick them on the fridge with a magnet. Ask God to help them always do what is right.

Killers forgiven!

26 Mar

"I forgive them for what they have done." Sometimes you hear this on a news report of a family tragedy. It is not an easy thing to say.

Read Luke 23:32–35.

What exactly does Jesus say? Jesus knows this punishment is an injustice. He does not deserve to suffer like this. However, he refuses to be bitter or resentful or hateful.

Jesus forgives even the people who are killing him – the soldiers and the crowd!

Write on a strip of paper: Jesus says, "I forgive you."

Put the paper strip on your mirror. Every time you look at yourself today thank Jesus for suffering on the cross and for forgiving you.

Who said what?

27 Mar

People still disagree over Jesus. Here three men say very different things to him.

Read Luke 23:36–43.

Use Codebreaker 1 on page 48 to work out who said what.

Soldier: FNIR LBHEFRYS VS LBH NER GUR XVAT BS GUR WRJF

Thief 1: FNIR LBHEFRYS NAQ HF

Thief 2: ERZRZORE ZR WRFHF JURA LBH PBZR NF XVAT

What does Jesus say to Thief 2?

Even though Jesus was in such pain, he was still kind to others.

Jesus' love is amazing and

____

____

_____________________________.

Thank you, Jesus.

The darkest day

28 Mar

Stormy clouds or an eclipse of the sun can make the daytime very dark! But this day was dark for other reasons too.

Read Luke 23:44–49.

Jesus had filled people's lives with hope, and now he was dead. Imagine how his friends must have felt. Lonely, hopeless, what else? Add your thoughts to the list.

hopeless

lonely

Draw a cross surrounded by storm clouds. Write some of your unhappy feelings on the storm clouds. Colour them with dark colours. Now remember Jesus' friends standing in the darkness looking up at the cross.

Talk with God about that.

Showing respect

29 Mar

Have you ever been to a funeral? Friends show respect and honour for someone they have loved with a solemn ceremony.

Read Luke 23:50–55.

How did Joseph of Arimathea show his respect for Jesus?

____

____

How did the women show their respect?

____

____

Both Joseph and the women were being very brave and kind. It was the custom to bury people with spices and perfume.

Do something extra kind today, to show your respect for someone.

Ask God to help you to be kind and brave even if you don't feel like it.

He can't lie!

30 Mar

What can't God do?

Check out Hebrews 6:18.

So... when God says something, it's true!

Here are some things God has said and some questions. Look up the verses and then join them together to answer the question.

How do I know that God loves me?

1 John 1:9

I'm doing something new and scary. Will God help?

Joshua 1:9

Is God with me all the time?

Hebrews 13:5

John 3:16

If I'm sorry, will God always forgive me?

I'm afraid! Help!

Psalm 23:4

Alive!

31 Mar

Do you remember "the darkest day" on Friday? Now get ready for an incredible surprise!

Read Luke 24:1–8.

Jesus is not dead – he is alive again! Wow!

Jesus had told his friends, "I will be killed, then come back to life." But they only understood him after it had happened. Before then it had seemed impossible.

Unjumble the surprises...

The stone door had been: **drello yawa** ____________________

The dead body was: **ont ereth**

____

Two messengers appeared in: **inshing scolthe** ____________

Imagine how the news headlines would report the story.

Thank God for this amazing miracle, that Jesus is alive!

Who will you tell?

Spread the news!

1 Apr

Have you ever had such good news that you just can't keep it to yourself? Mary and Joanna were bursting to tell the others. Then Peter rushes off to check it out for himself.

Read Luke 24:9–12.

Can you spot eight differences in these two pictures?

The good news has spread from the first Easter morning to today in exactly the same way. Who told you about it? Who will you tell?

Dear God, your message is such good news!

Thank you for __________ who told me about you. Help me to tell __________ about you too.

Lots of questions

2 Apr

Sometimes when you don't understand something, you have lots of questions. Some of Jesus' friends were upset and confused.

Read Luke 24:13–21.

What events are the two friends talking about? How do you think they felt?

Even though they were confused, things would turn out OK, and Jesus was still with them.

Imagine you were walking with Jesus. What questions would you have wanted to ask him? Write some of them down here.

____

____

____

____

____

Read your questions to Jesus now. If there's someone you trust who could help you answer these questions, talk to them too!

☐

Help with answers

3 Apr

Are you good at explaining difficult things? It's great to have someone to help!

Read Luke 24:22–27.

What does Jesus remind the two friends about? Circle the right answers.

Things written in scripture

To check their email and text messages

The Messiah had to suffer

Words spoken by prophets

A postcard they received.

Jesus used all the Old Testament to help his friends understand. What have you learnt from the whole Bible through using **Snapshots**?

____

____

____

Ask God to help you find answers to your questions. Say thank you for the Holy Spirit, for the Bible and for friends who can help you.

☐

It's Jesus!

4 Apr

What is it like when a friend or relative turns up unexpectedly to pay a visit? Perhaps you don't recognise them at first. What a surprise!

Read Luke 24:28–35.

What a shock it must have been! They recognise the "stranger", and then he leaves!

What do you think helped the friends recognise Jesus? The two friends hurry back to Jerusalem to tell the others.

(Psst! Emmaus is about 11 km from Jerusalem, nearly two hours of walking!)

Who else does Jesus visit? (See verse 34.) How many different people meet Jesus in Luke 24?

Dear God, thank you that Jesus surprised everyone by coming back to life!

Thank you that you are still with us today by your Holy Spirit.

It's no joke!

5 Apr

Have your friends ever told you to prove something you were telling them?

Read Luke 24:36–43.

How did Jesus prove to the disciples that he really was alive?

He showed them his __________ and ______ (verse 40)

He took a piece of fish and ____________ (verses 42–43)

Jesus wasn't tricking the disciples. This was for real. He had been raised from death. Impossible? Not for God!

I praise you, God, because nothing is impossible for you. You raised Jesus from death and he is alive now!

Thank you that it's no joke – it's for real, and it's for ever. Amen.

Amazing promise

6 Apr

Before Jesus died, he had told his disciples what would happen.

Read Luke 24:44–49.

Find these words of his in the wordsearch:

Messiah suffer death rise
father forgiven nations

R	M	E	S	S	I	A	H
E	P	O	S	W	E	R	H
F	O	R	G	I	V	E	N
F	A	I	T	H	F	U	L
I	V	E	H	T	A	E	D
S	N	O	I	T	A	N	N

Write down the leftover letters in order to find out what Jesus promised his disciples:

_ _ _ _ _ from _ _ _ _ _ _.

Jesus wants to give us his power, too, so that we can tell others the good news of Jesus.

Think of one person you would like to talk to about Jesus. Ask God to help you.

Believe it or not...

7 Apr

Have you ever been told something important, but not believed it? Thomas hadn't been there when the other disciples discovered Jesus was alive, so he didn't believe it was true. Write what he said when he did see Jesus.

Read John 20:24–29.

Tick the ways which help you to believe in Jesus:

- ☐ Reading the Bible
- ☐ Praying
- ☐ Being with people who believe in Jesus
- ☐ Knowing that Jesus is "My Lord and my God"
- ☐ Seeing God at work in people's lives
- ☐ Other ____________________

Only pray this prayer if you really mean it!
Please, Jesus, be my Lord and my God wherever I am and whatever I'm doing, especially when ________________________.

Inside information

8 Apr

Do you have a passport? If you don't, you'll probably have one when you're older. The Passport Office will want to know all about you.

Read 1 Corinthians 15:1–7.

In today's verses Paul tells the people in Corinth (a city in Greece) all about Jesus.

Can you number these facts about Jesus in the right order?

- ☐ Jesus was raised to life.
- ☐ Jesus appeared to more than five hundred other followers.
- ☐ Jesus was buried.
- ☐ Jesus appeared to his disciples.
- ☐ Jesus died for our sins.

What phrase is written twice in verses 3–7? __________________.

Paul was not making this up. The Old Testament scriptures pointed to what would happen. The New Testament completes the story.

Sing any song you know which says that Jesus is alive.

Whats the point?

9 Apr

Does anyone ever say to you: "What's the point?" Perhaps they are talking about some school-work, or a game you are playing.

In today's verses Paul talks about what the point was of Jesus coming back to life.

Read 1 Corinthians 15:12–14.

Read verse 14 again and then finish this statement. If Jesus was not raised from death...

____

and ________________________ .

That's how important the resurrection is!

Find a place where you can shout out loud. Say these words five times; loudly, softly, excitedly, happily and slowly...

"Jesus! You're alive!"

Same again!

10 Apr

Do you know people who say the same thing several times? That's what Paul does in his letter to the people at Corinth!

Read 1 Corinthians 15:17–20.

Paul wants to be sure everyone understands that, because Jesus rose from the dead, anyone who believes in him will also be raised to live in heaven for ever.

Can you put verse 20 into your own words? If you find this hard, talk about it to the person who gave you **Snapshots**.

Ask Jesus to comfort anyone you know who is sad because someone they love has recently died. If you don't know anyone, then pray for people in the world who are grieving now.

Body talk

11 Apr

Our bodies don't always work as they should. Sometimes it's because we don't treat them properly, but often there's nothing we can do about it and they won't last for ever. But... there's some brilliant news in today's verses!

Read 1 Corinthians 15:42–44.

Do a body check: How many cuts and bruises have you got on your body right now? What bit of your body doesn't always work perfectly? Do you have an illness right now? Yes/No

If we believe in Jesus, what will we have in heaven?

New bodies that are b_ _ _ _ _ _ _ _ and s_ _ _ _ _ (verse 43).

Thank God that in heaven he will give each of us a new body. There will be no illness or pain!

More of the same!

12 Apr

(Psst! If you are using the Good News Bible, "mortal" means that something dies, "immortal" means it goes on for ever.)

Read 1 Corinthians 15:52–53.

Paul is doing it again! He's telling the Corinthian people the same brilliant news again because he wants to be sure they understand!

Cross out all the xs to find out what will happen at the end of time.

Wewxillxallxbecxhanxgedxsox

thaxtwewxillxnevxerdieaxgaixn

Pray for someone you know whose body doesn't work properly. It may be someone with special needs in your class at school. Ask Jesus to keep them brave.

Victory!

13 Apr

If a team or a player you support wins an important match, what do you shout?

Read 1 Corinthians 15:54–58.

What has been destroyed and lost the battle (verse 54)?

Who has the victory (verse 57)?

Because Jesus died on the cross, we can win over s _ _ and d _ _ _ _ !

What do you want to shout now?

Use some of the words you have written in the speech bubble as a prayer of thanks to God

Puzzle time

14 Apr

The missing letters from the body parts will tell you the letters for the numbers in this code. Complete the grid and work out the words.

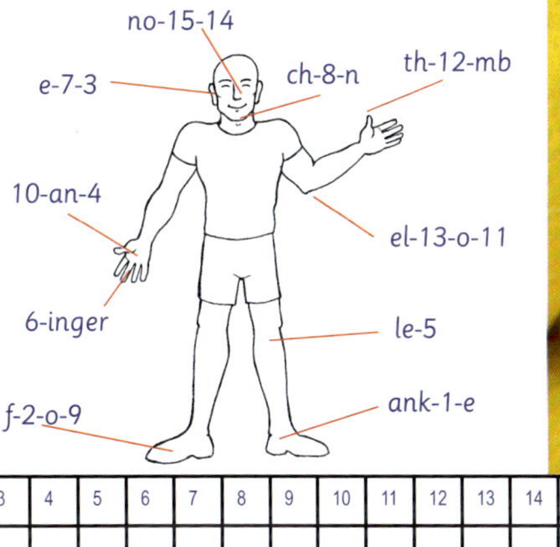

1	2	3	4	5	6	7	8	9	10	11	12	13	14	15

Thomas replied, "You are my 1-2-3-4 ________ and my 5-2-4_____!" Jesus said,

"Thomas, do you have 6-7-8-9-10_________ because you have seen me? The people who have 6-7-8-9-10 _________in me 11-8-9-10-2-12-9 _____________ seeing me are the ones who are really 13-1-14-15-15-14-4 ___________________!"

Check the answers by reading John 20:28–29.

That's not true

15 Apr

At the start of the Bible you can read how God made the universe and the very first people. They lived in a beautiful garden called Eden where they had everything they needed.

Read Genesis 3:1–5.

The snake tells Eve a lie to get her to eat from the forbidden tree. This is called tempting.

What did the snake say would happen if Eve ate the fruit?

Have you ever told a lie to try and make someone believe what was not true? How did you feel? Or has someone told you a lie? How did you feel then? Lies can hurt people, but sometimes they seem more exciting than the truth.

Say sorry to God for times when you have told lies. Ask him to help you always speak the truth.

Uncovered!

16 Apr

Sometimes we know straight away that we have made a bad decision.

Read Genesis 3:6–7.

The moment Adam and Eve ate the fruit they knew it was wrong because they knew things they did not know before. Realising they were naked in front of God made them feel very uncomfortable and so they covered themselves up. There are many things we can try to hide from God.

Think hard about something that you wish God didn't know about. Write it in the fig leaf in pencil. Read what you wrote to God. God already knew about it, but he is pleased that you shared it with him. When you have prayed, rub out the words. God has forgiven and forgotten them.

It wasn't me

17 Apr

Taking the blame is a hard thing to do. Often we pass it on to others and hope that we will get away with doing something wrong. Let's see what happens when God questions Adam.

Genesis 3:8–13.

Adam blames Eve and Eve blames the snake. They both try to say that it wasn't their fault, but we all have to take responsibility for our actions.

Adam and Eve had done the only thing that God asked them not to do. How do you think God felt? Write three things in the prayer below.

Dear God, when Adam and Eve did not listen to you I think you would have felt __________, __________, and __________. At times we can all let you down. Help me to be strong and do the right thing. Amen.

Judgement

18 Apr

Have you ever been punished for doing something wrong? Read about how everything on earth is punished.

Read Genesis 3:14–19.

God's punishments were:

The snake would crawl on its ____________ and eat ____________________(verse 14).

The snake and the woman would _________ each other (verse 15).

Eve will suffer pain when giving ___________ (verse 16).

The ground will be under a _____________ (verse 17), which will produce ___________ and ________________ (verse 18).

Draw Adam and Eve's faces when they heard these punishments.

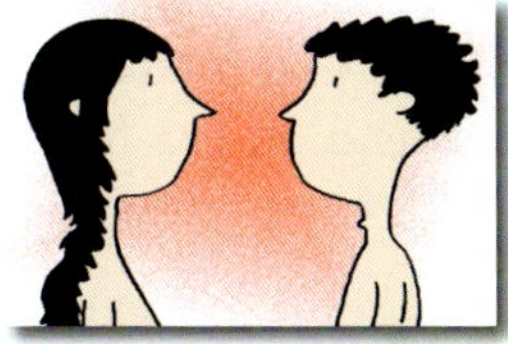

Lord, we know that you are a loving and caring God and that you want us to live your way. Help us to be like you. Amen.

God Still cares

19 Apr

Adam and Eve have been punished for doing wrong. Will God care what happens to them now?

Read Genesis 3:20–21.

Even though God was let down by Adam and Eve, he made them clothes to keep them warm. He doesn't stop loving people who disobey him.

Take a small bit of paper and write the words "God always cares" on it. (Put it in code if you like.)

Decorate the paper to make it bright and colourful. Fix it somewhere you will see it every morning – next to your bed or on the mirror in the bathroom. Remember every morning that God cares for you.

Thank you, God, that your love is so big that you never stop caring for me. Amen.

Punishment

20 Apr

Can you remember what the snake promised Eve? Was it true?

Read Genesis 3:22–24.

The snake had lied, and Adam and Eve were punished for trusting him instead of God. What did God do? (Fill in the missing vowels.)

H_ s _ nt th _ m _ _ t _ f
th _ g _ rd _ n

How did God make sure they didn't come back?

Draw a picture.
(Hint – check verse 24.)

God is a forgiving God, but he doesn't ignore our sin. When we do wrong, we deserve to be punished. Say sorry to God for times when you ignore him and go your own way.

True story 2

21 Apr

There was once a toyshop keeper named Mr Brown and a boy named Oscar. Oscar worked for Mr Brown and helped with deliveries. But instead of delivering the toys he often stole them. Then Oscar stole money from the shop and left town with his family.

Years later he returned and wondered if Mr Brown was still around. Oscar found the shop and went inside. Mr Brown was behind the counter. He recognised Oscar and rushed to greet him.
"But, Mr Brown..."

"It's all right, Oscar. I forgave you a long time ago," said Mr Brown. That's what God's grace is like. He forgives people for doing bad things even though they don't deserve it.

Have you asked him to forgive you? Can you find a story Jesus told that was a bit like this in Luke 15?

Who are you?

22 Apr

The Pharisees were Jewish leaders. They tried to obey God's laws in every detail. They even made up extra rules to help them not to break the laws. Jesus and the Pharisees had many arguments.

Read about a Pharisee who visited Jesus.

Read John 3:1–3.

Nicodemus was fascinated by Jesus and he wanted to find out more. What did he know about Jesus already? (Unscramble the words.)

EH ASW A TCRHEEA NEST YB OGD EH OUCLD OD RIMSELCA

(The answers are on page 192.)

What else do you know about Jesus?

Interview someone you trust. Ask them, "What do you know about Jesus?"

As Nicodemus talked with Jesus, he was in for some surprises. Ask Jesus to surprise you this week as you learn about him.

How to enter

23 Apr

Are you a member of any groups or clubs? What did you have to do to join?

Nicodemus was a Pharisee. Pharisees believed that obeying a lot of rules would make them God's friends, so Nicodemus was a bit surprised by what Jesus told him...

Read John 3:4–8.

Fit the correct words into the spaces. Jesus said:

"You can only ________________ God's ______________ by being ________ of __________ and of the _________________."

Spirit kingdom born
enter water

It's not what we do, it's God who makes us his children.

Draw a picture or find a photo of yourself and write this prayer invisibly with your finger on it:

Thank you, God, for making me your child.

How do you know?

24 Apr

Imagine that your friend gets hurt at school while you're playing. The teacher wants to know what happened. You can tell her because you were there.

Nicodemus asked Jesus how he knew so much about God.

Read John 3:9–13.

Where had Jesus come from? Use the first letter of each picture to check your answer.

_ _ _ _ _ _

Jesus knew all about God because he'd been with him from the beginning.

How else do we know that Jesus was with God from the beginning? Read John 1:1–2.

☐

Mission impossible

25 Apr

"Your mission, should you choose to accept it..." Have you ever seen a movie where the hero was given a special job to do? What was Jesus' special mission?

Read John 3:14–17.

More than a thousand years before this, God's people in the desert sinned and were bitten by poisonous snakes. God told Moses to hold up a metal snake on a pole. Everyone who looked at the snake was cured.

Who was going to be like that snake on the pole and cure people of sin? Cross out all the Xs and Zs:

Jesus came so that we WXOZNX'T ZDXIZE

But instead we have EZTXEZRXNZAXL ZLXIZFXE

Jesus came not to JXUZDXGZE XUZS

But instead to SXAZVXE ZUXS

Praise God, in your favourite way, for his gift of eternal life.

☐

Light versus dark

26 Apr

Have you ever seen an insect fluttering towards a light at night? Are you like that insect?

Read John 3:18–21.

Who lives in the dark? Give them a dark border.

Who lives in the light? Give them a light, bright border:

Those who do good things.

Those who do bad things.

Where do we get the power to do good things? Check verse 21 and write your answer in fancy writing in the spotlight.

Dear God, please help me to live in the light by obeying you and doing good things.

Tell me more

27 Apr

What has Nicodemus learned about Jesus so far? Imagine that he has sent you to find out even more.

Read John 3:31–36.

Finish the postcard to Nicodemus, telling him three things about Jesus from today's verses.

Dear Nick,

HEAVEN MAIL

Guess what! I've found out even more about Jesus!

He's __________________ And he is __________________

And __________________

Amazing!

Love from __________________

Think about all you have learned about Jesus this week. (Perhaps look back at each day to remind you.) Has anything surprised you? Share your thoughts with God.

Not them

28 Apr

Everyone asks Jesus for help, but in this reading Jesus asks for help. And he asks a very unlikely person.

Read John 4:1–9.

Who did Jesus ask to give him a drink?

A S _ _ _ _ _ _ _ _ _ w _ _ _ _

What did she reply?

'H _ _ c _ _ y _ _ a _ _ m _ f _ _ a d _ _ _ _ _?'

A man didn't usually talk with a woman alone. The Samaritans and Jews did not get on. (Find out why on page 69.)

This woman wasn't a 'good' woman. So Jesus was doing an amazing thing talking to this Samaritan woman!

Jesus cares about what people are like inside, not where they come from or what other people think of them. Everyone can be his friend.

Living water

29 Apr

What do you like to drink on a hot day when you're really thirsty?

Does it quench your thirst or just make you want more?

Read John 4:10–15.

What did Jesus say that his water will give? Cross out all the letters that aren't blue.

Pour yourself a drink of water. As you drink it, thank God for giving you eternal life (and enjoy your water!).

Do you think the woman understood what Jesus was telling her? How do you know?

Keep reading this week to see how she gets on!

How do you know

30 Apr

Fill in this FACT FILE about you.

Name:
Date of birth:
Country of birth:
Male or female:
Family members:
Favourite colour:
Hobbies:
Friends:

Does anyone else know all these things about you?

Read John 4:16–19.

Fill in the woman's FACT FILE:

Country of birth:
Male or female:
Number of husbands:

Jesus knew everything about the Samaritan woman even though they'd only just met. Jesus knows all about you, too, even things you don't know about yourself. Ask God to help you see yourself the way he sees you.

Peace

1 May

Do you think the woman Jesus was talking to had enjoyed a peaceful life? Probably not. But she was looking forward to the day that God would send someone special who would bring peace to the earth.

Read John 4:25–30.

Who did Jesus say that he was? Colour in all the spaces that have a dot to check your answer.

The Messiah means "the anointed one" or "God's chosen servant". People had been looking forward to him coming and changing their world for good.

What made the woman think that Jesus was the Messiah?

Dear God, please help people who especially need your peace.

Hungry for God

2 May

What's your favourite thing to do? Have you ever been so busy doing it that you've forgotten to eat your tea?

Read John 4:31–34.

What did Jesus say was like food to him? Starting at the letter "T", go round the circle in a clockwise direction, writing down every other letter as you go.

THOTOGBSELYBGPOADVAFNKDIDYOJHDIESRWQOURHK

_ _ / _ _ _ _ _ / _ _ _ / _ _ _ /
_ _ / _ _ _ / _ _ _ _ .

It wasn't that Jesus didn't need to eat! It was just that doing what God wanted was more important to him than anything else.

What's important to you? Where does God fit in? Talk to him about it.

How do you know?

3 May

Imagine that your friend has just told you that an alien has landed in his garden! What would make you believe him?

Read John 4:39–42.

Did the Samaritans believe what the woman said about Jesus? Some learned about Jesus by listening to the woman, others by meeting him.

Do you ever think of Jesus as your Saviour?

☐ yes ☐ no

Do you ever think of Jesus as the Saviour of people you don't like, or people in another country?

☐ yes ☐ no

What did the Samaritans come to believe about Jesus? (Check using Codebreaker 2 on page 48.)
He's the Saviour of the ?]@+$

Dear Jesus, help me to be certain that you're my Saviour and that you died for the whole world.

Enemies

4 May

There's a mystery over how Samaritans and Jews started fighting.

The Jews say that about 2,700 years ago some Jews were taken captive by the Assyrians and sent to another country. They married with local people and worshipped other gods, so they were not true Jews anymore.

The Samaritans say that their ancestors were pure Jews who either stayed in Israel or returned there afterwards.

It seems that the Jews told the Samaritans that they weren't pure Jews so they could not build the temple.

The Samaritans became angry and built their own place of worship. But the Samaritans claim that they built their temple at the place that Moses was told to worship.

Jesus accepted Jews and Samaritans, and encouraged his followers to do the same.

Stepping out in faith

5 May

Have you ever moved house? Finding a new house, packing, doing the legal paperwork, renting a removal van, unpacking, fitting into a new community... the list is endless!

It was very different for Abram more than three and a half thousand years ago...

Read Genesis 12:1–5.

Did God tell Abram where he was going? **Yes/No**

Did God explain how long the journey would take? **Yes/No**

Did God promise to bless Abram? **Yes/No**

Abram stepped out in faith, following God without knowing where he was going or what might lie ahead.

Draw around your foot, then cut out the shape. Write a one-line prayer on it, such as:

"Father God, help me to trust and follow you as Abram followed you."

Abram worships

6 May

How many churches are there in your town? They were built to honour God. Years ago, Abram wanted to build something for God. He built up a huge pile of rocks and offered one of his best animals to God. This rocky monument was called an altar.

Read Genesis 12:6–9.

Look at the picture clues and put the correct letter in each box.

☐ Abram built his first altar here.

☐ Abram built a second altar here.

☐ This place was his final destination.

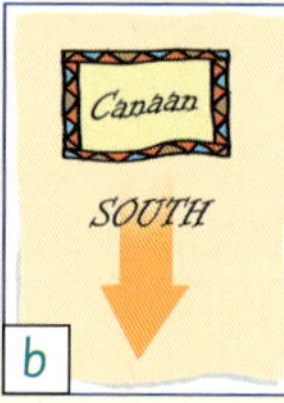

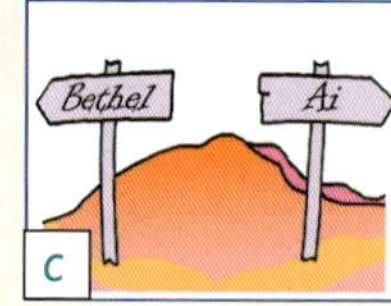

Abram worshipped God everywhere he went. Where do you normally talk to God? Why not choose a different place today?

Travelling and trust

7 May

What's the best thing about your home?

Abram was a rich man and probably very comfortable at home, but God said "Time to move on!" What did Abram do?

Read Genesis 13:1–4.

Can you find the good things that Abram owned, listed in verse 2, in this wordsearch?

(Look out for three types of animal and two precious metals.)

H	G	C	E	W	O	B
G	O	A	T	S	R	E
S	L	T	O	H	I	T
I	D	T	L	P	A	H
S	I	L	V	E	R	E
S	H	E	E	P	A	L
P	E	D	G	O	S	D

Find Sarai and Lot and the place where Abram was heading in the wordsearch. The leftover letters say what he did when he got there.

_ _ / _ _ _ _ _ _ _ _ _ _ _ / _ _ _

Lord, no matter how rich and comfortable I become, help me to be always ready to follow you.

Making up

8 May

There was one cake and two brothers. They quarrelled until Mum told the older boy to cut the cake in half and let his brother choose which half he wanted. Abram has to sort out a quarrel in today's Bible story. Watch out for the answers to these questions:

Who was fighting?

Why were they fighting?

What did Abram decide to do?

Who seemed to do best out of this arrangement?

Who was more generous?

Read Genesis 13:5–11.

Why do you think this story is in the Bible? What do you think God might be trying to tell you through it?

Lord, sometimes it's hard to be fair. Please help me to be a peacemaker who's willing to compromise a little, to act generously and to make a fresh start.

Against the odds

9 May

A little time has passed since Abram and Lot separated. When a battle took place in the land chosen by Lot, Abram (with God's help) came to his rescue and brought him to safety.

Read Genesis 15:1–6.

What three things did God promise he would do for Abram? Look at each picture and say aloud the promise.

Abram was an old man so it must have been hard for him to trust God to keep his promise, but he did.

Father God, you have promised us new life and a place in heaven. Help us to trust your promises just as Abram trusted the promises you made to him.

New name

10 May

Have you ever had a nickname? Perhaps a name with a special meaning like Speedy or Goldilocks? God gave Abram a new name...

Read Genesis 17:1–8.

Abram means 'exalted Father', but God wanted to give him a new name. Add the correct letter in the gap. ABRA _ AM

What did this new name mean? Circle the right answer.

Loyal Father Loved by God

Father of Nations.

In verse 6, God promises that Abram's descendants will include kings. Look up these verses then write the name of each king on the crown.

2 Samuel 5:3 1 Kings 1:39 Luke 1:31–33

Lord, thank you that your plan for the world went from Abraham to Jesus. Thank you that you have a plan for my life too.

☐

A warm welcome

11 May

Tick the good things to do with visitors to your home.

- ☐ Open your door with a smile.
- ☐ Offer them a seat.
- ☐ Spend time chatting.
- ☐ Share a meal.
- ☐ Something else? ____________

Read Genesis 18:1–8.

Number these events 1 to 6, in the order that they happened.

Abraham:

- ☐ bowed down
- ☐ brought water to wash their feet
- ☐ ran out to meet them
- ☐ asked Sarai to make bread
- ☐ asked a servant to cook
- ☐ served the food himself
- ☐ offered them rest in the shade of a tree.

Abraham's three visitors were not human at all! Who do you think they were?

☐

Amazing but true!

12 May

Which of the following are just a giggle and which are totally true...

1. Minnie Munro got married in Australia at the age of 102.
2. Fred Hale was issued with a driving license at the age of 104.
3. William Baldwin crossed a canyon in America by tightrope on his 82nd birthday.

Find the answers on page 192.

Read Genesis 18:9–15.

Why was Sarah laughing?

Use Codebreaker 2 on page 48 to find out how the Lord replied.

(# ![_~*([& ~]] *!@$
^]@ ~*% +]@$

Psst! Have you noticed that God has also changed Sarai's name – she is now Sarah, which sounds a bit like the Hebrew for "Mother of Nations" (Genesis 17:15).

Amazing Lord, thank you that you created our wonderful world and you created me. Nothing is impossible for you.

The promise arrives

13 May

On a scale of 1 to 5, how patient are you? 1 is mega-patient and 5 is impatient. Circle your answer.

You are given a birthday present a week early. Do you open it or wait? 1 2 3 4 5

You friend is half an hour late. Do you wait for them?

1 2 3 4 5

You're reading a book and can't wait to find out how it ends. Do you sneak a look at the last page?

1 2 3 4 5

Sarah had to wait patiently for years for God's promise to come true.

Read Genesis 21:1–8.

What was the child called?

____

How old was Abraham when the baby was born?______________

How did they celebrate?

____

Thank you that you answer prayers when the time is just right. Help me to be patient as I wait for your answer.

Proving his love

14 May

In Bible times, people would take something special – things like fruit, wine or a young animal – and offer it to God on an altar.

This was called making a sacrifice. It was a way of saying thank you to God for all the good things he provides.

Read Genesis 22:1–8.

What incredibly hard thing does God ask Abraham to do?

Does Abraham do this willingly?

God doesn't ask Abraham to do anything that he isn't willing to do himself. Years later he sacrificed his own son Jesus so we could be his friends. Look up John 3:16.

Lord, Abraham trusted you with the life of his son. Help us to show even a fraction of his trust.

The Lord provides

15 May

God has provided us with many good things for which we can be thankful. List as many things as you can think of.

Read Genesis 22:9–14.

Can you number these pictures in the right order?

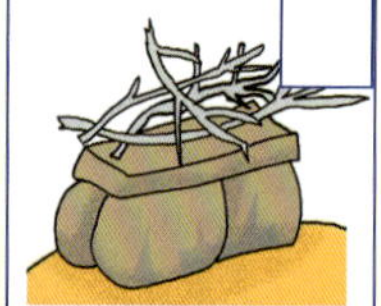

Abraham showed that he put God first in his life when he was willing to give up his son. God stopped him, but why do you think he asked in the first place? Talk about it with someone who knows God.

Ask God to help you trust that he knows best whatever he asks of you.

The promise renewed

16 May

When Paul Brand was a young doctor he obeyed God's call to work with people with leprosy, a skin disease. Because of his work, millions of people all over the world have been helped.

Look out for who would benefit from Abraham's obedience in today's passage.

Read Genesis 22:15–19.

God promised to _ _ _ _ _ Abraham.

He said Abraham would have as many descendants as there are _ _ _ _ _ in the sky or grains of _ _ _ _ on the seashore.

God was pleased that Abraham _ _ _ _ _ _ him.

Abraham was even willing to give up his only son _ _ _ _ _.

Abraham finally settled in the town of _ _ _ _ _ _ _ _ _ _.

Thank you that you kept your promise to bless Abraham and his descendants. Please bless me too.

Good question!

17 May

Did Jesus see the pyramids? Every tourist who goes to Egypt visits the pyramids! They were built 5,000 years ago out of huge stone blocks.

No one's sure how the stones were moved without modern technology. The pyramids were tombs for the pharaohs – the kings of Egypt.

The biggest one is just outside the capital city, Cairo, and it's 147 metres high – that's three times higher than the Statue of Liberty, and half as tall as the Eiffel Tower!

You can even go inside some of them. It's only spooky if the lights go out!

Egyptian Christians are very proud that Jesus visited their country. Maybe Jesus saw the pyramids when he was a baby!

I will be with you!

18 May

Jesus had gone back to heaven to be with God, but he promised the disciples they would not be alone...

Read Acts 2:1–4.

Can you complete this headline?

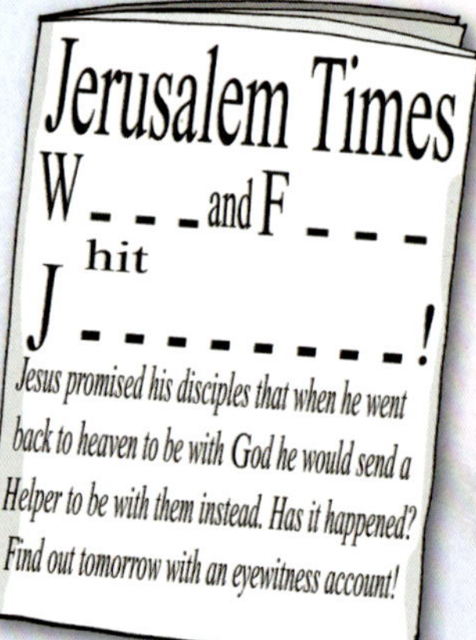
Jerusalem Times
W _ _ _ and F _ _ _
hit
J _ _ _ _ _ _ _ _ _ !
Jesus promised his disciples that when he went back to heaven to be with God he would send a Helper to be with them instead. Has it happened? Find out tomorrow with an eyewitness account!

Thank you, God, that all through the Bible you promise to be with your people. Thank you for the Holy Spirit who is with us all the time.

Amen.

What does this mean?

19 May

When something hits the headlines, there are often statements from people who saw it happen – just like today's verses.

Read Acts 2:5–13.

Now read today's **Jerusalem Times**.

Jerusalem Times
Eyewitness accounts of yesterday's events!
Reports that believers were drunk have yet to be confirmed.
A visitor from Asia said, "We heard fishermen speaking to us in our own language, but people from other countries could also understand them. I can't explain it. They were praising God, so maybe it had something to do with him."
Another visitor from Greece (who did not wish to be identified) asked, "What does this mean?"

When the Holy Spirit came at Pentecost, people from many different countries heard about Jesus.

What does your church do to help people in other countries hear about Jesus? Can you find out?

Not drunk!

20 May

A drunk person often seems happy (for a while). Some people said the disciples were drunk because they were so excited about what had happened.

Read Acts 2:14–18.

Now join the right questions and answers together:

Questions:

- Who stood up to speak to the crowd?
- What did he call the crowd?
- What did he say about the disciples?
- What time was it?
- What had God done?

Answers:

- Fellow Jews/ Friends
- Nine o'clock in the morning
- Poured out his Spirit on his followers
- They are not drunk!
- Peter

Lord God, thank you that the Holy Spirit helped the disciples to be brave so that they could tell everyone about Jesus. Thank you that the Holy Spirit is our helper and friend, too. Amen.

All in God's plan

21 May

When David wrote the psalms he never expected that hundreds of years later Peter would quote his words from Psalm 16:8–11 to a crowd of thousands! Look it up later.

Read Acts 2:22–28.

What did Peter explain to the crowd? (Use Codebreaker 2 on page 48 to help you.)

God had {+![[%$ that Jesus would be *![$%$]>%@ and put to death][! £@]##.

God would @!(#% *(= ~] +(^%.

Why? So he could £][}<%@ $%!~* for ever!

Tell God how you feel about this.

A psalm comes true!

22 May

When God sent his Holy Spirit, the words of **Psalm 16:8–11** came true! If you didn't have time yesterday, read it now.

Read Acts 2:32–33.

32 All of us can tell you that God has raised Jesus to life!

33 Jesus was taken up to sit at the right side of God, and he was given the Holy Spirit, just as the Father had promised. Jesus is also the one who has given the Spirit to us, and that is what you are now seeing and hearing.

Draw a straight line under the words that say that Jesus is alive.

Draw a wavy line under the words that say Jesus went back to heaven to be with God.
Circle the name of the person God promised to send instead of Jesus.

Use the words of Psalm 16:8–9 as a prayer of thanks to God.

Turn away from your sins

23 May

Peter's message to the crowd was simple and clear. Read what happened when they heard it...

Read Acts 2:37–39.

Fill in what the people asked in verse 37:

Then what happened? To find out, read verse 38 again clearly and loudly, as if you were Peter answering their question.

If you are like the people who asked, "What shall we do?", pray this prayer (if you really mean it), even if you have already taked to God like this before.

Father God, I'm sorry for the things I do wrong that do not please you. Thank you that Jesus died for my sins so that I could be forgiven. Please help me to turn away from my sins and turn back to God. Send your Holy Spirit to be with me. Amen.

Power

24 May

What's the most powerful thing you've ever seen? A hungry shark's jaws? A crashing waterfall? A jet engine?

Some of the most powerful things in the world cannot be seen. When did you last see electricity? We can see what electricity does when it lights up a Christmas tree, or a computer screen, but we can't see the electricity itself.

And what about the wind? It's only air after all, and air's invisible, right? But there's no doubt it's real – ask someone whose roof has just blown off! We can't see what it does.

Light and sound waves are in the air all around us and most of the time we don't even think about them. Mobile phones pick up invisible signals, so do TVs and radios.

Isn't it amazing that things we can't see have such a big effect on us?

☐

Sharing God's glory

25 May

After Jesus went back to heaven, Paul went everywhere spreading the message of Jesus, starting new churches.

He wrote letters to help churches understand about Jesus and live for him. The one he wrote to the church in Rome we call "Romans".

Read Romans 5:1–2.

Tick three things Paul tells them.

- ☐ We have been put right with God through faith.
- ☐ Jesus is alive in heaven.
- ☐ We will share God's glory.
- ☐ We have peace with God through Jesus.
- ☐ "God's grace" is a way of saying that we experience the "undeserved kindness" of God?

Give thanks to God we don't need to be perfect to earn his love and forgiveness.

☐

Last the distance

26 May

Top athletes put up with pain and tiredness so their minds and muscles become stronger and they can perform even better.

Find out how to take on life's troubles like a top athlete (even if you're not at all sporty).

Read Romans 5:3–5.

Trouble can have good results. Trusting God when things are bad can help us get stronger and trust him more. He helps us to _ _ _ _ _ _ .

Find the letters with the red dots.

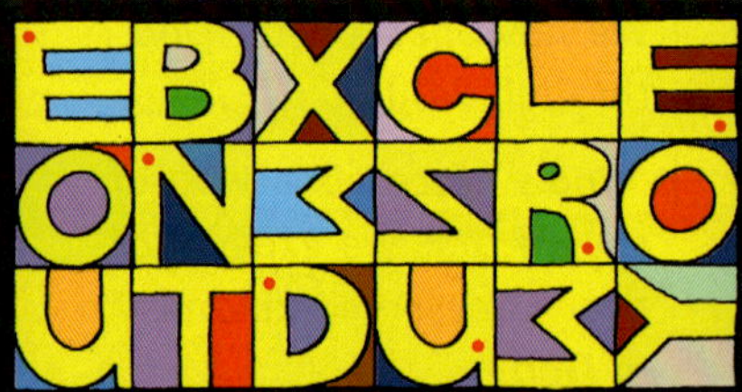

Ask God to continue to support you in troubles so you can endure. Sit quietly and feel his love around you.

Saved!

27 May

Everyone does wrong things sometimes. But God didn't only choose the good people to do something special for.

Read Romans 5:6–8.

When did Christ die for us?

When we were

____

____

Read that again. That's amazing!

God didn't wait for us to be good before he did something to rescue us. God was willing to let his Son die for people, even though they didn't care about him.

Try learning Romans 5:8 off by heart. Teach it to the person who gave you **Snapshots**.

Thank God for forgiving you, even before you knew him.

Shake hands

28 May

Has anyone who used to be your enemy become your friend? What changed?

Read Romans 5:9–11.

Fill in the missing words – *friends, sacrifice, anger, enemies.*

Because of Christ's _ _ _ _ _ _ _ _ _ we are saved from God's _ _ _ _ _.

We were God's _ _ _ _ _ _ _ _, but he made us his _ _ _ _ _ _ _ .

Friends with the creator of the universe? Amazing! And all because of Jesus.

Lord God, thank you for making me your friend.

Not guilty

29 May

Imagine you are in court. You expect to spend the rest of your life in prison for your crimes. Then you hear the judge say, "Not guilty!"

Read Romans 5:14–16.

Sin came into  through A _ _ _ .

Ever since Adam everyone has been **GUILTY** of sin.

God's  came through J_ _ _ _ C_ _ _ _ _ _.

God's  is that we're **NOT GUILTY**.

Jesus' one pure life overcame years and years of sin. Thank God that Jesus takes away your sin so you're not guilty.

One man

30 May

If you are sick you might have to see a doctor who will give you some medicine to get rid of the illness and make you better. Paul tells us how Jesus got rid of the illness of sin and made us right.

Read Romans 5:17–19.

Circle the things that Jesus' death does:

Makes us free

Makes us sad

Gives us life

Makes us God's enemies

Puts us right with God

Let's us rule in life

Makes us sin

Over the past week we have been reading about the amazing thing God did for us when he sent his Son to die for us. What's the best way you can think of to praise God for that? Do it!

Prayer time

31 May

Sometimes it's hard to know what to pray about... at other times we may just forget to pray.

Try this handy reminder ("handy", get it!)

Lay your hand out flat and hold one finger at a time. Pray for each of these five subjects, one at a time.

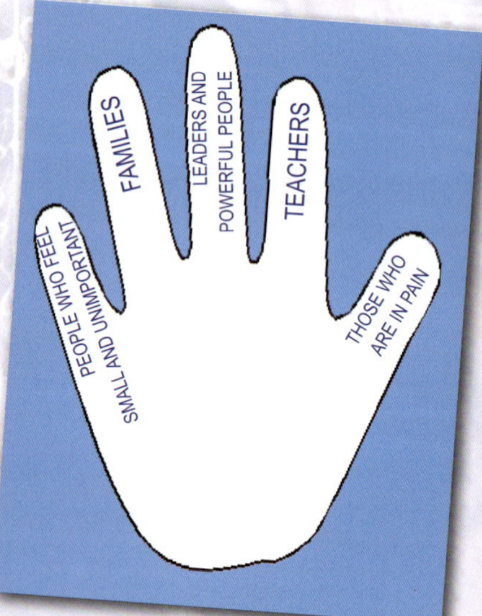

The challenge!

1 June

How tall are you? Imagine what someone who was 3 metres tall would look like and how you would feel if he was challenging you to fight!

Read 1 Samuel 17:4–11.

Here is a picture of Goliath.

Unscramble the words and draw on him all the things that we know he was wearing.

Zrbeno mruora

_ _ _ _ _ _ / _ _ _ _ _ _

Ozrbne mlheet

_ _ _ _ _ _ / _ _ _ _ _ _

Ezbnor inveaj

_ _ _ _ _ _ / _ _ _ _ _ _ _

What would make you volunteer to fight the giant?

Think of a time when you were afraid. Tell God how it felt. Ask him to give you his courage.

Meet David

2 June

Today's reading is about someone from Bethlehem. Who do you know who was born there?

Read 1 Samuel 17:12–19.

Looking after sheep was a dangerous job. You might be attacked by lions or bears. Circle the words that you think describe David.

Do you think God wanted David to hear Goliath? Why/why not?

Dear God, I know that you have a plan for me. Help me to listen out for what you want me to do. Amen.

Send me!

3 June

Do you ever feel that because you are not an adult some people don't listen to you properly? If they said, "You're just a kid, what would you know?", how would you feel?

Read 1 Samuel 17:26–33.

David's brother Eliab says three things to him. What are they?

1 __________________________

2 __________________________

3 __________________________

Are there times when people ignore your ideas because you're young? Can you think of any good ways to make sure your opinions are heard at school, at home or where you live?

Ask God to give you confidence to speak out when you think that something important needs to be heard.

Lions and bears!

4 June

In the time of David there were no planes or guns. People used heavy swords and wore lots of armour to protect them from their enemies.

Read 1 Samuel 17:34–40.

Circle "Yes" or "No".

David had been in battle lots of times. Yes/No

The Lord had protected David from lions and bears. Yes/No

David knew he was representing the army of the living God. Yes/No

Saul refused to let David fight because he was too young. Yes/No

We know what Goliath wore into battle; look back at your picture on page 83. In the box draw what David took into battle with him.

David must have been scared, but he had confidence in God's power. Ask God to give you confidence to represent him.

Secret weapons

5 June

David marched into battle with just a sling and five stones to face Goliath in all his armour.

Read 1 Samuel 17:41–47.

Goliath laughs at David because he is so young and carries no weapons, but David has a secret weapon that Goliath doesn't know about.

Look for David's weapon in these Bible verses, then crack the code (using Codebreaker 2 on page 48) to check your answer.

~*%   [!=%]^   ~*%
+]@$!+=!&*~_

Thank God that we know about his great power and ask for his help to share it with others.

The fight!

6 June

Do you know the story of the hare and the tortoise? Everyone thought the hare would win because hares run faster. But it didn't because the tortoise was smarter!

Who do you think will win between David and Goliath?

Read 1 Samuel 17:49–51.

David brought the 3-metre-tall man to the ground! Being strong and tall does not always mean you win!

How do you think that David felt when he won? Who should David thank for winning the battle? Pretend that you are David and write a prayer on the shield thanking God that you won and telling him how you feel.

Heroes of prayer

7 June

As well as killing a giant, David was a great writer and musician and he sang prayers to ask God for help, to thank him and to praise him.

Sometimes he just wanted to tell God that he loved him. He really wanted to know God better. Here's one of his prayers.

Read Psalm 42.

Now fill in the missing words:

As a ____ gets ______

for ______ of _____,

I truly am ______ for you, my God.

In my _____, I am _______

for you, the ______ God.

Which word appears more than once in David's prayer? Do you ever feel "thirsty" for God? Ask him to help you love him and want to know him better every day.

Jealousy hurts!

8 June

Jealousy is when you are angry with someone because they can do something you can't or have something you don't. Can you think of a time when you felt jealous?

Read 1 Samuel 18:6–11.

What made King Saul feel jealous? What did Saul do?

The Philistines were a warlike people who often attacked the Israelites to take over their land. When David killed Goliath he saved Saul's kingdom at least for a while.

Dear God, forgive me for the time that I felt jealous towards __________ because _________. Please help me to be grateful for all you have given me. Amen.

Jealousy kills!

9 June

Do you think Saul started to feel better and learned to love David again? Read on!

Read 1 Samuel 19:8–12,18.

Fit these words in the spaces – kill, spear, harp, wall, threw.

David was playing his _ _ _ _ .

Saul had a _ _ _ _ _ in his hand

Saul _ _ _ _ _ it and it stuck in the _ _ _ _ .

David ran, but Saul sent men to _ _ _ _ him.

If David's wife hadn't told him to run away, what do you think might have happened?

God often works through other people to help us. Thank God for some of the people that help you to avoid danger.

In hiding!

10 June

Have you ever hidden under the bedcovers when you were scared? David was scared that Saul would kill him, but he had to hide further away than that.

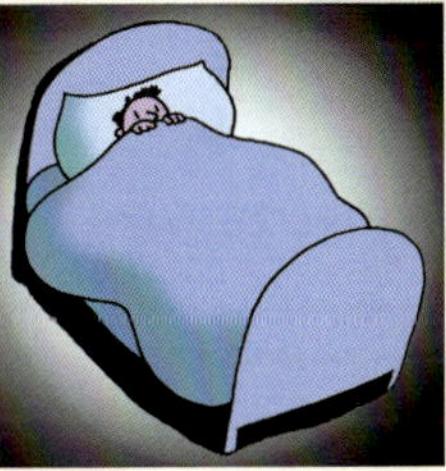

Read 1 Samuel 23:14–15.

David had to be careful to stay hidden. Do the verses tell us how he felt? Circle the ones you think he felt:

Happy Scared Lonely

Excited Joyful

All the time David was in the desert, in fact his whole life, someone more powerful than King Saul was watching over him. We know who that was don't we?

Can you think of people who might be feeling afraid at the moment? Ask God to help them know that he is watching over them right now.

Revenge?

11 June

When someone has been nasty to us, we might feel like getting back at them, making them feel as bad as we did.

Saul was trying to kill David, and now David gets his chance for revenge.

Read 1 Samuel 24:1–7.

Tick the right answers.

Saul took 300 ☐ 3,000 ☐ men with him.

He walked into the same cave ☐ house ☐ that David was hiding in.

David's men wanted him to welcome ☐ kill ☐ Saul.

David would not because God had chosen Saul to be king ☐ God had told him not to in a dream ☐ .

Thank God for a time you did what God wanted even though it was hard.

☐

Forgiveness rules!

12 June

There are many ways to show that you forgive someone for something they've done to you. We know that David did not kill Saul when he had the chance.

Read 1 Samuel 24:8–11.

In which verse do you find the following:

David bows to Saul – verse ___ .

David shows Saul the piece of his robe he cut – verse ___ .

David asks why Saul listens to people who say he is trying to kill him – verse ___ .

David tells Saul he has done him no wrong – verse ___ .

When David runs out of the cave he calls out to Saul. What does he call him? Rearrange the letters –

j m y r a e t o s u y

____

Thank you, God, that you give us the power to be loving and forgiving, even to people who don't deserve it.

☐

The Lord bless you!

13 June

This story has reached an exciting point. Saul now has David standing in front of him explaining that he could have killed him. What will Saul do?

Read 1 Samuel 24:16–22.

True or false?

When David finished speaking, Saul was angry. **T/F**

Saul knew that David was right and he had been wrong. **T/F**

Saul knew that David could have killed him. **T/F**

Saul knew that one day David would be king of Israel. **T/F**

Saul recognised that David was a great man. What did he ask David to do for him?

Lord God, I pray that you'll bless anyone who doesn't like me.

David's message

14 June

David became King of Israel and did many great things and was rich. But he also disobeyed God and took someone else's wife.

Then he put her husband in a very dangerous place during a battle so he would be killed. The story continues... God sends a message to David...

Read 2 Samuel 12:1–4.

The story the prophet told has a hidden meaning for David. Can you think what it might be?

How do you think the poor man felt when his only lamb was taken?

What kind of person do you think the rich man was?

In what way was he like David?

Ask God to help you understand this message.

The message explained!

15 June

Yesterday we heard a message sent from God to David. You might want to go back and read the message again before we hear what it means.

Read 2 Samuel 12:5–10.

Who was the rich man in the message? ___________

List the four things that God had given David.

____

____

What was the name of the man who David had killed in battle?

____

The Lord says that something will happen to David's descendants. What is it (verse 10)?

____

What a message!

At times we all disobey God, even though we have been given so much. Can you think of a time you've disobeyed God? Talk to God about it now.

David's song

16 June

As we found out on 7 June, David wrote songs and poems called psalms. He wrote this one after Nathan had given him God's message.

Read Psalm 51:1–5.

Have you ever fallen and got a grass stain on your clothes? It makes an awful mess and it's very hard to wash out.

The evil that David did is his dirty mark, his sin. He can't get rid of it. He is asking God to wash it away and make him clean again.

Pick out some words that show David knows he's done wrong.

Can you write a poem or a song like David's? Try – you might surprise yourself.

Get rid of it!

17 June

David feels bad about his sin and continues to ask God to forgive him.

Read Psalm 51:6–13.

Find the answers:

What does God want (verse 6)?

____

What does David ask for (verse 8)?

____

What does David ask God to create in him (verse 10)?

____

What does he ask God not to take away (verse 11)?

____

When David has asked for all these things he promises to do something for God. What is it (verse 13)?

____

Ask God to give you joy and gladness and a pure heart. Ask for help in all that you do for God.

Humble before God

18 June

In the time of David people took offerings or sacrifices of birds or animals to the Temple, sometimes to thank God and sometimes to say sorry. These became burnt offerings in the Temple fire.

Read Psalm 51:14–17.

David knows that burnt offerings will not help him get on the right track with God again.

What does God want?

Write the words from verse 17 here.

Thank God for his forgiveness, no matter what you have done.

Consequences!

19 June

Throughout Psalm 51, David has asked God for mercy. How will God respond?

Read 2 Samuel 12:12–15.

Nathan passes on this important message to David. Decode it with Codebreaker 2 on page 48.

~*% +]@$ ^]@&(>%# _]<
_]< ?(++ []~ $(%

____

____

David is forgiven but there is still a consequence. Something bad will happen because of what he did. Find it in verse 14.

(Psst! Not everything bad that happens is because of disobedience. Accidents and illness happen too. And God cares whenever anyone dies.)

What about this?

20 June

One day, my brother Charlie was upset. He said he didn't feel that God talked to him much. We explained to him that God talks to people in different ways.

You don't always hear things. Sometimes it's ideas through art, sounds, pictures and things like that.

Charlie told us that he had asked God whether his mum or dad loved him. In his mind he got a picture of a red heart but he wasn't sure what it meant. We told him that a heart means love.

Then we had a prayer time, asking God to help Charlie to feel loved and to recognise when God was speaking to him.

All this time the weather outside was stormy and miserable, but when we finished praying there was the sun, poking out through the clouds. And there was not one rainbow, but two!

We all felt that God was powerfully showing us he loved us in a special way.

A letter from God!

21 June

This week we are reading from some letters that God asked John to write to early Christian churches in Turkey. God tells them some surprising things!

Read Revelation 3:1–6.

God says three things:
(unscramble the letters)

kewa pu! ____________________

embremre ____________________
what you were taught.

nutr romf ___________ your sins.

Find some coloured paper and cut out seven stars. Stop and think about some of the things you have learnt about following God and living right. On each star write one thing to remember. Then stick the stars around your mirror (or somewhere else you will see them every day).

Ask for help to remember the things you have learned, so you will always honour God in the way you live.

A key to unlock doors!

22 June

Imagine you are in a beautiful palace with lots of rooms, but some doors are locked. Can you get in? Who has the key?

Read Revelation 3:7–8.

What happens when God opens a door? What happens when he closes it?

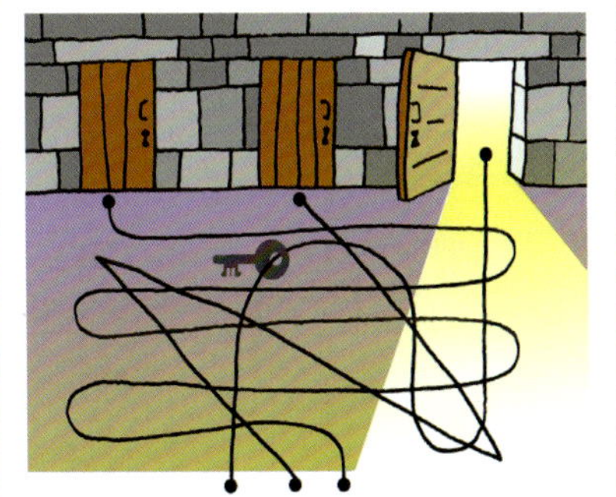

Only the person who has the key can let you in! God promises to open doors for his faithful friends, so we can come to him.

Thank you, God, that I can come and talk to you anytime.

Every time you see or use a key today, ask yourself: am I living faithfully to God?

Hang in there

23 June

Think of some tough situations you have had to go through. How much easier is it when you have a good strong friend with you to help you out?

Read Revelation 3:9–10.

Think about what God might be saying to you through this, then use Codebreaker 2 on page 48 to work these out:

You]”%_%$.

You %[$<@%$

God +]>%# you.

God will {@]~%£~ you.

God is the strongest, most faithful friend to those who stick by him!

Tell God about some of the tough situations you have to face. Remember God's promise to be with you, especially when things are difficult. Say thank you to God.

God's new name

24 June

Sometimes people have the name of their friend or hero or a person they love tattooed onto their body. Once you have a real tattoo you can't wash it off! It is there for ever!

Read Revelation 3:11–13.

One day God will write his name on you! Why do you think God wants to do this?

Is it because... (Tick as many as you think are true.)

- ☐ God loves you?
- ☐ You belong to God?
- ☐ God thinks you are a hero?
- ☐ You will be with God for ever?
- ☐ You are God's friend?

Did you know that God's people are like a temple? We'll never be made of real stones and pillars, but together we make a place where God is worshipped.

How do you feel about God giving you his name? Tell him about it now.

Spit it out!

25 June

Hot chocolate and chilled lemonade – we love them both! But no one likes hot chocolate that's gone cold or warm lemonade on a hot day! Ugh, it makes you sick!

Read Revelation 3:14–19.

People who follow God should be... Hot with eager energy for right living and cool with willing obedience. But not half-hearted and uncommitted. Measure where you fit on the scale:

loving God

helping others

obeying God's word

telling others about God

listening to God

If you are lukewarm, how could you change today? Think about it! Ask God to help you to be eager to live right and willing to obey.

Lunchtime

26 June

Imagine Jesus calling round to have lunch with you and your family and friends. What would you say to him?

Read Revelation 3:20–21.

These are really important words! Jesus wants to be part of your life and to spend time with you. And he promises that you can spend time with him too. You are welcome in his kingdom.

Do you want to open the door and let him in? If you do, pray a prayer like this one, and tell the person who gave you this **Snapshots** that you have prayed it.

Dear God, I can hear your voice calling me to follow you. Please come in and be my friend for ever. Amen.

Codebreaker 3

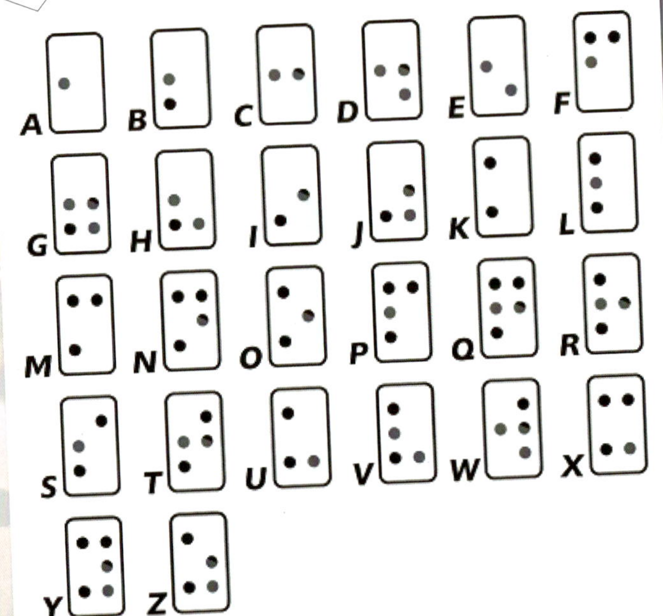

Codebreaker 4

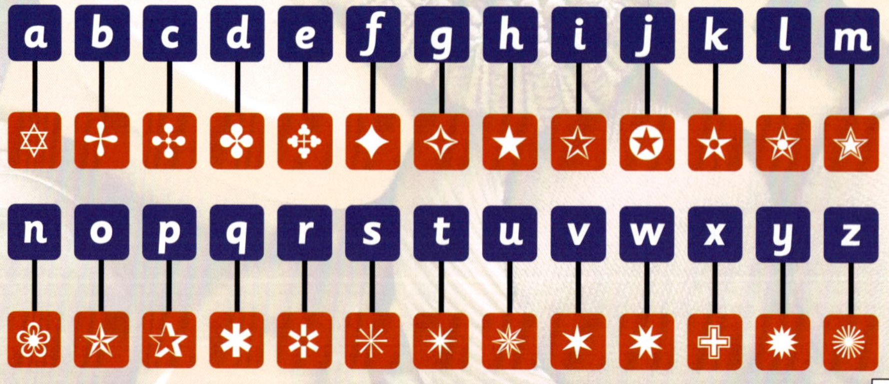

Taken to Babylon!

27 June

King Nebuchadnezzar had attacked Jerusalem and taken prisoners back to Babylon. Now he needed some men to serve in his palace.

Read Daniel 1:1–6.

What sort of men was Nebuchadnezzar looking for? (verse 4)

What were they to eat? (verse 5)

How long did they have to train for? (verse 5)

What did they have to learn? (verse 4)

The king gave lots of orders – but who was really in charge of everything? (Verse 2 might help.)

It must have been hard for Daniel and his friends to be taken to a foreign country. Ask God to help you stay close to him when life gets hard, and to keep doing what pleases him.

Ten days of cabbage!

28 June

Have you ever been told to do something you know God wouldn't want you to do?

Read Daniel 1:8–16.

Daniel wasn't just being fussy! The food they were given had been dedicated to Babylonian gods, so in God's rules it wasn't allowed. Unscramble the words to find out what they had instead:

GABLEVSEET OT TEA

____

TREWA OT INKDR

____

How were they ten days later?

____________ and ______________ than everyone else.

Would you be able to keep God's rules when everyone around you was doing something else? Read about someone who did what was right, like Daniel did, on page 100.

Ask God to help you stick up for what you know is right.

"What can you do?"

29 June

Does your teacher give you a report to take home at the end of the school year? It was a bit like that for Daniel and his friends.

Read Daniel 1:17–21.

Put a circle round what they were good at:

running
reading (skill in literature)
maths
philosophy (being wise)
science (understanding dreams)
cookery
knowledge

Who gave them all these gifts?

____

Thank you, God, for all the gifts you've given me, especially

______________________________ .

Later, Daniel would use his gifts to help the king. Who can you help with your gifts?

Impossible!

30 June

Have you ever been asked for an answer when you didn't know what the question was?

Read Daniel 2:1–6.

What was the king's problem?

He had a _ _ _ / _ _ _ _ _ _ .

Dear God, it's horrid when I have a bad dream or when I'm feeling afraid at night. You promised to be with us always – so please help me to know that you're there with me, looking after me.

The king had lots of helpers in his palace. Who do you go to when you have a problem or need advice? Why not make a thank you card for someone who helps you?

Daniel's wisdom

1 July

Think of a time when you've used one of the gifts God has given you. Now was the time for Daniel to do the same...

Read Daniel 2:10–18.

Fill in the missing vowels to find two wise things Daniel did.

W_NT T_ T_LK T_ _R_ _CH (verse 14)

_SK_D F_R M_R_ T_M_ (verse 16)

Daniel knew that only God could answer King Nebuchadnezzar's impossible question – so what did he ask his friends to do? PR_Y (verse 18)

Is there anything for which you need God's help? Like Daniel, you could ask some friends you trust to pray, too. What happened after Daniel's friends prayed? Read verse 19.

Only God can

2 July

If Daniel tells the king that he can interpret the dreams he could be rich and famous (see Daniel 2:6). What do you think Daniel will do?

Read Daniel 2:26–29.

Daniel spoke up for God.
Fill in the speech bubbles.

Man can't do it, but _ _ _ in _ _ _ _ _ _ reveals and explains _ _ _ _ _ _ _ _ _ _ .

What was the dream about?

God told you what will _ _ _ _ _ _ in the future.

Look at verse 47. King Nebuchadnezzar was amazed by God. What do you think of God? Tell him.

Football Swearing!

3 July

When I first went to secondary school, I felt a bit like Daniel when he was in Babylon. I really wanted to live for God and I knew almost everyone else at school wouldn't understand!

Each playtime and lunchtime we played football.

One thing that older boys can be really bad at is swearing and using bad words. Before I became a Christian, I used to swear a lot, but after I became a Christian, I knew this had to change so I asked for God's help.

Every time I felt myself wanting to swear, I deliberately told myself not to and trusted God to help me. He really did help, even though my friends kept swearing. I knew I was doing what God wanted me to do and I was pleased that my friends accepted that I was a bit different and we just got on with it!

Dave Godfrey

Daniel does his duty

4 July

Have you ever been given a special job to do?

Daniel was now working for a new king. How would he get on?

Read Daniel 6:1–3.

Cross out every fourth letter. What job was Daniel given to do?

INCXHARXGEOXF THXEGOXVERXNORXS

____

How well did he do his work?

VERXYVEXRYWXELL

____

Then what position did the king give Daniel?

INCXHARXGEOXFTHXEWHXOLEX KINXGDOXM

____

Why do you think Daniel was so good at his work?

Ask God to help people who lead – for instance teachers, church leaders – to be wise, fair and loving in the decisions they have to make.

A cunning plan

5 July

Have you ever felt jealous of someone? How did it make you behave towards them?

Read Daniel 6:4–9.

Here is the king's decree. Unfortunately some of the words have been partly rubbed out. Can you finish it?

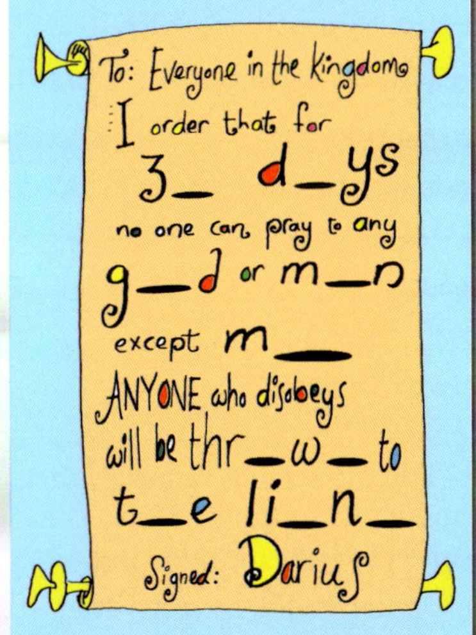

Why were the governors jealous of Daniel?

If people tried to find fault with you, what would they find?

Dear God, help me to be reliable, good and honest like Daniel.

In the open!

6 July

Imagine you've been told that if you read **Snapshots** you'll not be allowed to watch TV for a month! What will you do?

Read Daniel 6:10.

Join the dots to find out where Daniel prayed.

Why do you think Daniel didn't pray in secret?

Despite the dangers, Daniel stayed faithful to God. Even today, in some countries it's dangerous to be a Christian. Ask God to keep believers safe and to help them to stay faithful to him.

Do people at your school know you love God? If they do, how do they know? If they don't, why not?

Sneaky supervisors!

7 July

Has anyone ever told tales about you?

Read Daniel 6:11–16.

The governors had got what they wanted! The king had made a law and so he had to obey it.

Did the king want Daniel thrown to the lions? How do you know?

King Darius knew how much Daniel loved God. Use Codebreaker 3 on page 96 to find out what he said:

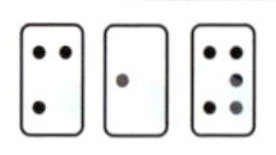

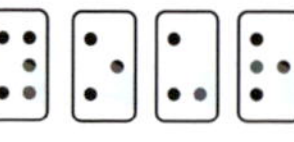
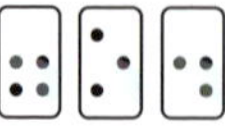

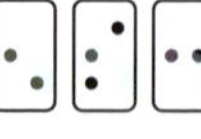
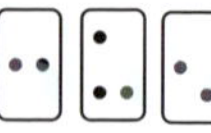

Use these words from Psalm 46 as a prayer. Try making movements to the words to help you remember them:

"God is our shelter and strength, always ready to help in times of trouble."

Lion food?

8 July

What's the scariest place you can imagine? Imagine how Daniel felt!

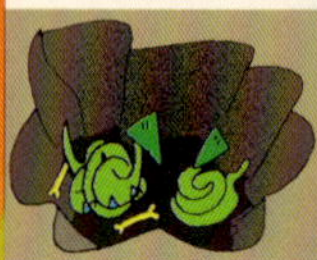

Read Daniel 6: 17–23.

True or false?

The king left the pit uncovered. T/F

No one could rescue Daniel. T/F

The king slept well. T/F

Angels shut the lions' mouths. T/F

The next morning the king was very anxious. T/F

Daniel trusted God to save him. T/F

(Answers on page 192.)

God can save people, even from impossible situations. Using the word "SAVED", write a prayer like Daniel might have written. It's been started for you...

Strong and mighty God

Always there

V

E

D

Who's the real God?

9 July

Imagine you've just discovered something wonderful. What do you do?

Read Daniel 6:25–28.

King Darius had found out all sorts of things about God. He wanted to tell the world.

Fill in the chart with words from his letter.

What God's like	What God does
Living	Rescues

Daniel's faith had influenced the king. Who might your faith be influencing?

Use the king's words to help you praise God. If you can make up a tune, sing the words.

Spot the difference

10 July

Can you find five differences between these two pictures of Daniel and the lions?

Jesus wants to heal

11 July

Imagine having disgusting spots and scabs on the back of your hand. How would you feel?

Read Matthew 8:1–4.

What was this man's problem?

Imagine...

what he looked like
how he felt
how he thought Jesus would feel about him

What did Jesus do? (Put a tick in the boxes.)

- ☐ gave him medicine
- ☐ touched him
- ☐ healed him
- ☐ prayed for him
- ☐ hugged him
- ☐ told him to obey Jewish laws
- ☐ told him to tell everyone
- ☐ said he wanted to help

Lord Jesus, thank you that you always want to help us.

☐

Jesus shows his power

12 July

Can you imagine what it must be like to see a tsunami coming? Find out what scared the disciples...

Read Matthew 8:23–27.

Add vowels to the waves to show what Jesus said to the disciples.

Close your Bible and tell the story. Here are some words to get you started:

Jesus and his disciples... Jesus was very tired so... They didn't expect... The disciples thought... So they... Jesus told them off because... Then he... Everyone felt...

What do you think was more scary – the storm, or Jesus' amazing power?

Tell Jesus about everything that scares you, and ask for his help.

☐

Jesus forgives and heals

13 July

List the things it would be impossible to do if you couldn't use your arms or legs. List things you could do.

Read Matthew 9:1–8.

Blasphemy = speaking carelessly about holy things or making insulting statements about God, like claiming to be God.

Jesus knew all that this man needed.

Take out the Qs and Zs to find what the teachers didn't realise.

Jqezsuqs hqadz zGqodqs qpozwqezr tqo qfozqrgzqqivqe sqiznsz

On a piece of paper, draw the outline of a person. Keep it. Over the next two weeks, we'll read about people who needed different sorts of healing.

Each time you read about Jesus healing someone, draw in the part that Jesus healed.

Jesus invites all

14 July

Is there anyone in your school who isn't very popular? Imagine or draw them in the diamond shape.

Read Matthew 9:9–13.

Matthew was a taxman and respectable people didn't like him because they hated paying taxes to Rome.

What did Jesus say to him?

Where did Jesus go?

What did the Pharisees grumble about?

Jesus didn't stick with the respectable people, those who thought they were already good enough. Circle the verse that tells who Jesus said he had come for.

9 10 11 12 13

Pray for the person in the diamond shape. How could you be friendly to them? (Play with them at break? Be their partner sometimes?) Ask Jesus to help you.

Loads of faith

15 July

Read about two blind men who believed that Jesus could heal them, so they asked him to...

Read Matthew 9:27–31.

If you're reading with at least two other people, act out the story. (Extra people could be the crowd.)

What's different about the faith in yesterday's reading and the faith in today's? (see page 192)

What problem do you need help with most of all? Do you believe Jesus can help? Imagine you are in the house with Jesus and these blind men.

If your faith is very small, ask Jesus for more faith. Imagine asking Jesus to help with your problem.

Jesus is with you. Pray about your problem now.

Good and bad power

16 July

Have you ever tried to explain away something so you didn't have to admit you were wrong?

Read Matthew 9:32–34.

The Pharisees saw Jesus drive out the demon but they still didn't want to say that Jesus was from God. Where did they say that Jesus' power came from?

Check your answer with Codebreaker 3 on page 96.

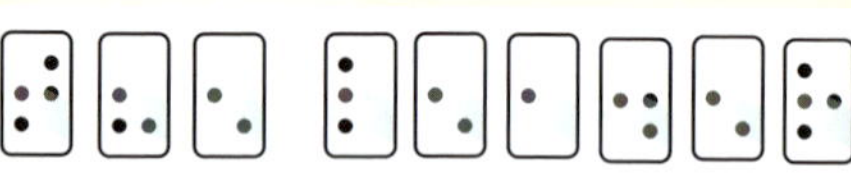

____

____

If you'd been there, what would you have thought? Would it convince you to follow Jesus? YES/NO

Lord Jesus, I praise you because you are much more powerful than the devil.

Jesus' big task

17 July

What do you want to do with your life? Jesus has a job for you!

Read Matthew 9:35 – 10:1.

Jesus' disciples went with him through country towns and villages. People needed to know that life would be different in God's kingdom. But they needed someone to tell them.

Jesus used a farming picture to explain. Match the description to the meaning:

Harvest

Christians willing to share the good news

Harvest workers

People ready to hear about Jesus

Jesus and the disciples started to bring in the kingdom harvest, but it's not complete yet.

How could you be a harvest worker for Jesus now? In the future?

Lord, please send harvest workers to _______________ to tell people about God's love.

It's no yoke

18 July

Some people have a very hard life. Jesus had a strange solution.

Read Matthew 11:28–30.

Join the dots.

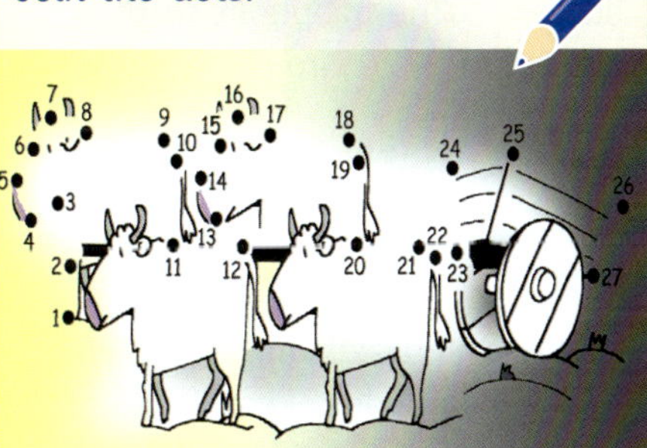

A yoke is a wooden frame to help farm animals pull together. If it doesn't fit, or the load is too heavy, the animals are uncomfortable.

Jesus promises us comfort if we work in a team with him.

Pray for anyone you know who finds life difficult. Pray that they will team up with Jesus and use his strength every day.

Love versus rules

19 July

Do you agree with this statement? Rules are like a straightjacket. Why?/Why not?

(A straightjacket is a type of harness to tie people in so they can't hurt or destroy things.)

Read Matthew 12:9–14.

The Pharisees had rules and lots of them. They had rules to stop people breaking rules! So that people would keep God's commandment to "Keep the Sabbath day holy", they had lots of rules about what you couldn't do on the Sabbath. You couldn't walk far, or gather firewood, or do any work.

So did they think it was OK to heal someone?

The Pharisees said: YES/NO

What did Jesus think? YES/NO

Lord Jesus, help me to recognise what's really important.

Safe and rescued

20 July

Fishermen go to work very early. Do you like to be up before dawn?

Read Matthew 14:25–32.

In pencil, draw Jesus very faintly at ↓ in the morning mist. Peter wanted to be sure, but he wobbled.

Draw Peter at ↓↓ beginning to sink. Go over the drawing of Jesus more firmly, and draw him reaching out to save Peter.

Talk with God about things that make your faith wobble.

What's your problem?

21 July

Do you see people around you with big problems? You may have seen refugees on the news or people caught in a flood or a drought. What if we could bring them all to Jesus?

Read Matthew 15:29–31.

Match up the opposites:

mute	seeing
crippled	walking
lame	speaking
blind	able-bodied

Find these words in the wordsearch: crowds, Jesus, bringing, feet, amazed, praised, many

F	R	I	E	N	P	D	S
H	E	L	P	M	R	E	D
J	E	S	U	S	A	E	A
B	R	I	N	G	I	N	G
C	R	O	W	D	S	C	Y
H	O	T	F	E	E	T	H
A	M	A	Z	E	D	E	R

Make a sentence with the leftover letters: _ _ _ _ _ _ _ _ / _ _ _ _ _ _ _ / _ _ _ _ _ / _ _ _ _ _

Jesus cares

22 July

Who makes your food? Buys your clothes? Puts a plaster on your grazed knee? Say thank you to someone who cares about you.

Read Matthew 15:32–38.

Sort out the numbers:

7   a few   4,000   3   7

_____ days in the desert

_____ loaves

_____ fish

_____ baskets of leftovers

_____ men

Look at both verse 32 and 9:36. How are they similar? Use Codebreaker 3 on page 96 to find out what they both say about Jesus.

Make an alphabetical list of things that God has given, and thank him for them, eg Apples, Bed, Cousins...

Total forgiveness

23 July

Would you forgive a friend who...

Told tales about you?
Borrowed a CD without asking?
Wrecked your bike?

Even when people say sorry, it's not always that easy to forgive...

Read Matthew 18:21–27.

How many times did Peter suggest he would forgive – 7, 9 or 11 times?

How many times did Jesus say would be better – 17, 77 or 490 times?

What do you think Jesus meant by this? Fill in the speech bubbles using verses 26 and 27.

Forgiving Father, thank you that when I am sorry you always give me a fresh start. Help me to show the same forgiveness to others.

Forgive and be forgiven

24 July

It's a great feeling to know you are forgiven.

Read Matthew 18:28–35.

Can you number these pictures correctly?

How is this like the Lord's Prayer about forgiveness? Check out **Luke 11:2–4.**

Think back over last week. Did you do anything to make God sad or angry? Ask him to forgive you.

Think ahead to next week. Ask God to help you to be ready to forgive others.

Making agreements

25 July

Have you ever been paid for washing the car? Weeding the garden? Vacuuming? Something else? Did you agree the price beforehand?

Read Matthew 20:1–7.

When did the man first go to the marketplace?

How much did he agree to pay the workers?

On these clocks, show the other times when he hired workers:

Lord, we need things to do each day. Please help those people who are out of work and looking for jobs.

Unexpected generosity

26 July

Sam has a swimming party and invites his whole class. He includes friends he's known for years and children who joined the class recently. How do you think his old friends feel?

I'm glad to be invited.

I wish he'd only invited a few old friends.

The more the merrier!

Read Matthew 20:8–16.

The men who started at 5 o'clock earned the daily rate even though they'd just started.
Draw how they felt.

The men who started at 9 o'clock earned the daily rate too.
Draw how they felt.

It doesn't matter whether you've loved Jesus for eight weeks or 80 years. Everyone who turns to him has a place in heaven. What do you want to say to God about this?

Dear Dave

27 July

Dear Dave

Is God male or female?

Lots of love, Alex

Dear Alex,

That is a very good question!

In the Bible, God is called "he". He is God the Father (male parent), God the Son (male child!) and God the Holy Spirit. Like a good father, God cares and provides for all his children.

There are some passages in the Bible which tell us that God is also like a really good mum!

Jesus talked about looking after his people like a mother hen looks after her chicks (Luke 13:34)!

Both males and females are made in God's image and are like him in lots of ways. God is quite different from human men and women. God isn't human at all. God is God.

Lots of Love,

Dave

Forgiven: a fresh start

28 July

Remember a time when you did something wrong, or messed up, or upset a friend. How did you feel about it?

God's people felt really down after they had badly messed things up and done wrong. But God sent Isaiah along with some messages to cheer them up!

Read Isaiah 40:1–2.

What words does God use? Circle them.

comfort compost contort condemn encourage enslave embarrass enchant

Make a scroll out of a long piece of paper, to take note of the messages God gives to Isaiah. Today's messages are: God comforts us, and God forgives us.

Tell God the things you are sorry for today. Say thank you for God's comfort and forgiveness. God promises you a fresh start!

Pathway of light!

29 July

Have you ever had to sweep a pathway clear of leaves or snow? Bulldozers can cut a roadway through almost anything! Isaiah is told to clear a road. Why? Who is coming?

Read Isaiah 40:3–5.

Today's message is in verse 5: the _____ of the _____ will appear! When the incredible majesty and beauty of God's great power appears, who will see it (verse 5)?

What do you think that moment will be like? Look at verse 4 again, then close your eyes and try to imagine it!

Now get your scroll (from yesterday). Add pictures of a clear road, and of all the people around the world seeing God's glory! Thank God for this amazing promise!

Wise words

30 July

Who do you know who you can really trust? Even your best friends today cannot always be there for you tomorrow! What are people like?

Read Isaiah 40:6–8.

Pick a flower from your garden (ask first!), and put it in a cup of water on your window ledge. How many days will it last in the sunshine?

Which of these living things will last for ever?

Write on your scroll: "God's Word lasts for ever!" Draw something to remind you.

Thank you, God, that we can always trust you. Your words are true and your promises last for ever. You really are amazing!

Mountaintop message

31 July

Imagine that you have just been told the best news ever! What could it be? Something so exciting that you want to shout it from the top of a mountain! Isaiah heard some news like that!

Read Isaiah 40:9–11.

Write these messages (not backwards) in your scroll, and draw a mountaintop for today's good news.

* !gnimoc si doG (verses 9 and 10)
* !lufrewop dna gnorts si doG (verse 10)
* !eltneg dna gnirac si doG (verse 11)
* !su retfa kool lliw doG (verse 11)

Share this amazing good news with a friend at school today. Dare you!

Dear God, help me to be honest with my friends about how amazing you are!

Like one of the stars!

1 Aug

Can you count the stars? There are millions. On a clear, dark night you can see thousands of them! When the sun sets, ask if you can go outside and have a look!

If it's cloudy, think of them shining brightly behind the clouds.

Read Isaiah 40:25–27.

What does this tell us about God?

If God cares so much about the stars and all creation, how much do you think he cares about people? Just like the stars, God created you! God knows all about you! God calls your name!

Add today's messages to your scroll, and decorate it with some stars all around the edge!

Energy like eagles!

2 Aug

Try running on the spot. How long can you keep going? Get a clock and time yourself. Imagine if you could run a whole marathon without getting tired!

Read Isaiah 40:28–31.

Some people seem to have lots of energy, but we all get worn out in the end! Where can we get energy and courage to always do the right thing? (Clue: see verses 29 and 31.)

On your scroll draw an eagle and a pair of running shoes!

Look at all the messages on your scroll. How do they make you feel? Tell God how you feel about them. Ask God for energy and courage to live right all the time.

You've said it!

3 Aug

Some people use the names of God and Jesus as swear words. Find out if those people are being led by God's Spirit.

Read 1 Corinthians 12:1–3.

What did you discover?

This part of the Bible started out as a letter that Paul wrote to Christians in the city of Corinth, in Greece. They used to worship idols, but now they were following Jesus. God's Spirit lived in them. Which verse is this picture about?

Listen for the words 'Jesus' or 'God' this weekend. The Holy Spirit will let you know if words are being used in the right way.

Ask God to help you be truthful about Jesus with your words. Pray for those who you hear swearing.

Lots of gifts!

4 Aug

Are you generous? Do you like giving gifts? God gives people lots of skills and abilities. God loves to give!

Read 1 Corinthians 12:4–6.

What things can you do? Where do your skills and abilities come from? It doesn't matter if you can't do what others can do.

God made you unique and different from others.

Link up the halves...

We can do different things	to serve the same Lord
There are different gifts	but the same God works in all I
There are different ways	which come from the same Spirit

Find a picture of yourself. As you look at it, say thank you for the gifts God has given you.

Fruit salad?

5 Aug

You can't make fruit salad with just one type of fruit! You need lots of different ones! Likewise, God gives lots of different gifts.

Read 1 Corinthians 12:7–11.

How many gifts can you find here?

X	S	H	Z	P	X	K	Z
Z	E	E	X	E	Z	N	G
X	L	A	Z	O	M	O	N
X	C	L	X	P	O	W	I
F	A	I	T	H	D	L	K
X	R	N	Z	E	S	E	A
Z	I	G	X	C	I	D	E
X	M	Z	X	Y	W	G	P
Z	G	N	I	V	R	E	S

What are some other gifts you might have? Encouraging others, doing maths, helping out, writing poems, learning languages, drawing pictures, or something else?

Thank you, God, that you give each of us different abilities. Help me to discover and use the skills you have given me.

Body parts!

6 Aug

Imagine you had five feet and no hands! Or three ears and no nose! How strange that would be!

Read 1 Corinthians 12:14–20.

God's family is like a body with different parts. If all the parts were the same, it would be a strange body!

Touch your eyes, ears, mouth, feet and hands. As you do, think about how you can use your body to help others.

Write a body poem, with a verse for each part of the body. Finish it by saying thank you that you are a special member of God's family.

Worth it!

7 Aug

How often do you get ignored? It hurts when we are treated as unimportant. But God never treats anyone like that!

Read 1 Corinthians 12:21–26.

This tells us that those of us who think we can't do much are still very important. To God, children are as important as adults. Weak people are as good as very strong ones. Slow thinkers are as good as brainy people.

Draw (stick men will do!) some of your friends, family and other people in your church. Now think of something you especially like about each of them.

Perhaps they are a good listener, or they are kind to you. Write these next to the pictures.

Say thank you to God for each one of the people you drew.

Super heroes?

8 Aug

Do you know a real live superhero?

Someone who can do everything?

Someone who can rescue the planet from disaster? Probably not!

Read 1 Corinthians 12:27–30.

Nobody can do everything, but everyone can do something.

Jesus Christ (in his body) did wonderful things when he was on earth. Now all his followers are his body. And he's in us! Together we do what he wants to do.

Ask God to show you what you could do for him. Try to think of something at home, at church, or at school. Then sit quietly and listen for new ideas from God.

Don't forget: you may need to ask permission from a carer, leader or teacher.

Ancient prayer

9 Aug

Lord, make me an instrument of your peace;
where there is hatred,
let me sow love;
where there is injury, pardon;
where there is doubt, faith;
where there is despair, hope;
where there is darkness, light;
and where there is sadness, joy.

O Divine Master,
grant that I may not so much
seek to be consoled as to console;
to be understood,
as to understand;
to be loved as to love;
for it is in giving that we receive,
it is in pardoning that we are pardoned,
and it is in dying that we are
born to eternal life. Amen.

(Often called a prayer of Francis of Assisi, but no one really knows where it first came from.)

Messages from God

10 Aug

Elisha lived in Israel about 850 years before Jesus. He was a prophet, which means that he gave messages from God to the people.

As you read about Elisha over the next two weeks, look out for different ways he communicated God's messages.

Read 2 Kings 4:1–4.

What was the only thing the woman had left in her house?

____

What were Elisha's first words to the woman? Write them in the speech bubble.

Elisha knew that God wanted him to help others. God would help him do that. Talk with God about how you can help people. Ask him to help you.

Saved!

11 Aug

Remember the poor widow in yesterday's story?

What was she going to do with all the jars she'd collected?

Read 2 Kings 4:5–7.

Fit the correct word from the list into the spaces...

OIL	FULL	MONEY
DEBT	LIVE	SOLD

All the jars were ________.

She ________ the _______ and paid the _______.

She had enough __________ left to ________ on.

Is there something you need God's help with?

Write it in the jars and then read it out loud to God.

God can do anything!

Rich people too!

12 Aug

Do you have a special guest room in your house?

Does the same person often stay in it?

Read 2 Kings 4:8–17.

Look again at verse 10 and add the furniture to Elisha's special room.

Elisha was grateful to the woman and wanted to do something in return. What did Elisha say God would do for her?

God knows what we need even better than we do!

Thank God for three things you need that he has given you.

Think of something you can do for someone who has helped you.

Tragedy strikes

13 Aug

Think of a time when life was great... and another time when life was really difficult. Sometimes things change without any warning.

The woman from Shunem had a child and life was wonderful. But then...

Read 2 Kings 4:18–25.

Something terrible had happened and the woman was desperate! She needed a friend, especially a friend who knew and trusted God.

Help the woman to find Elisha.

Who do you turn to when things go wrong?

"Thank you, God, for people who are there for me when life is hard, especially..."

Seven sneezes

14 Aug

What's the first thing you do when you've got a problem?

What did Elisha do as soon as he saw the boy?

Read 2 Kings 4:32–37.

Elisha needed God's help to know what to do, so he prayed. Write the word "Pray" in fancy writing.

What happened next?

God's power worked through Elisha in an amazing way.

The woman fell with her face to the ground as a sign of respect for Elisha (verse 37).

Think of three amazing things about God. Why not kneel down with your forehead touching the floor and praise him?

Don't eat that!

15 Aug

Have you ever smelt milk that's gone off or seen mouldy bread? Their smell and colour are warnings to show us that they won't taste good!

Read 2 Kings 4:38–41.

Cross out the wrong words:

There was no food/lots of food/party food in the land.

Elisha asked his friends to make toast/stew/a cup of tea.

The people said "It's poisoned"/"It's yummy"/"It's terrible".

Elisha threw in some flour/meal/chocolate.

The stew was pink/worse/fine.

God's power can make bad things good.

Talk with God about a bad situation that you would like him to make good. Ask him if he wants you to do anything about it.

Spots!

16 Aug

Have you ever had an infectious illness, like chickenpox? People keep away in case they catch it. Imagine what it would be like to be infectious all the time!

Read 2 Kings 5:1–6.

Draw a:

○ Around the person with the skin disease.

□ Around the person who wanted God to help him.

△ Around the person he went to visit.

▭ Around the person God used.

Who's got two shapes round them? God used a young, unimportant girl to help a rich, important soldier!

Talk with God about what he might use you to do for him. Remember to listen for an answer.

Seven soaks!

17 Aug

Do you prefer sitting in a nice, warm bath or standing under a refreshing shower?

How do you feel afterwards?

Read 2 Kings 5:7–12.

Fill in the missing vowels:

Elisha told Naaman to:

W_sh s_v_n t_m_s _n th_ r_v_r J_rd_n.

Naaman wanted Elisha to:

Pr_y t_ G_d _nd w_v_ h_s h_nd v_r N_ m_n.

Why do you think Naaman felt angry with Elisha?

God doesn't always work as we expect him to. Can you think of other times when God has worked in an unexpected way?

Next time you...

...wash your face, thank God for making you special.

...wash your hands, ask God to use you to help others.

No, thank you

18 Aug

What would you do if a teacher praised you for doing something you didn't actually do?

Read 2 Kings 5: 13–16.

Colour the gift red for true and blue for false.

Naaman did what Elisha told him.

Naaman bathed three times.

Naaman's skin got worse.

Naaman offered Elisha a gift.

Elisha wouldn't take the gift.

(Answers on page 192.)

Elisha hadn't made Namaan better. Who had healed Naaman and deserved his thanks? Write your answer on the gift tag.

Think of something God's done for you that a person couldn't do – and thank him.

No surprise!

19 Aug

It's no use trying to creep up on someone if they know you're coming.

The Syrian army wanted to ambush the Israelites. Read how the Israelite army found out they were coming.

Read 2 Kings 6:8–13.

Number the speech bubbles in the right order to tell the story.

☐ I want to capture him.

☐ Who told the enemy?

☐ It's Elisha! He can hear everything you say.

☐ Here's a good place to for an ambush.

☐ Don't go there!

How do you think Elisha knew what was happening?

Sometimes God's power works very quietly.

Sit completely still and quiet for a minute and then pray,

"Father God, help me to be a good listener – to you and to others."

Surrounded!

20 Aug

Look at this picture. What do you see? Two people looking at each other, or a vase? Ask someone else what they see.

Sometimes we can look at the same thing but see something different.

Read 2 Kings 6:13–17.

What could Elisha's servant see (verse 15)?

No wonder he was afraid!

So why wasn't Elisha afraid (verses 16–17)?

God's power is always there, even when we can't see it.

Dear God, help me to know that you are always with me, even when it feels like you're not there.

Fight or feast?

21 Aug

Have you ever been tempted to try and get your own back on someone who's hurt you?

Read 2 Kings 6:18–23.

Fit the missing words into the spaces:

The S _ _ _ _ _ army attacked Israel.

The Lord made the Syrians b _ _ _ _.

Elisha led them into Israel's capital city, S _ _ _ _ _ _.

The king wanted to k _ _ _ the enemy army.

Elisha said, "N _".

The king gave them a f _ _ _ _ and sent them h _ _ _.

God used his power to rescue Israel, not to harm the Syrian army.

What did the Syrian army do in return?

Lord, when people upset me, help me not to fight back but to think of good ways to stop the arguments.

Choice game

22 Aug

Challenge instructions:

Start on the red square and step to the green square.

You may go left, right, up or down (but not diagonally!).

After a yellow square you must choose a blue square.

After a blue square you must choose a yellow square.

Some useful advice:

Ali says choose yellow first

Ben says choose blue first

Whose advice did you follow?

Answer on page 192.

Just what I needed!

23 Aug

Can you think of a present you've been given? When you opened it, did you say, "That's just what I needed!" or, "I've always wanted this!"?

Read Acts 3:1–6.

Draw what the man asked for here:

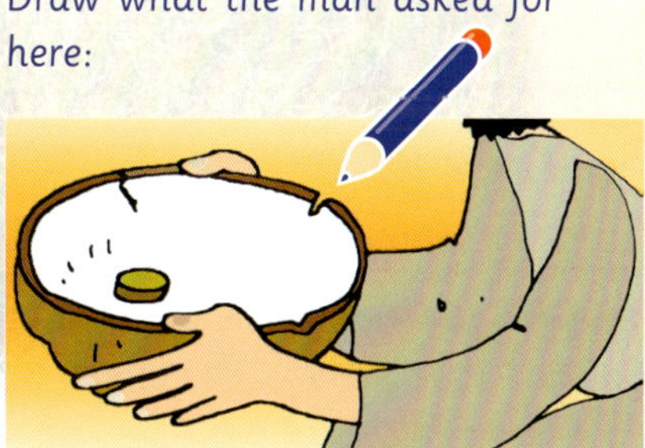

Peter and John knew what the man really needed, which was much better than money. What was it?

Check out verse 6.

When you pray this prayer, hold your hands as if you are begging like the lame man.

Thank you, God, because you always know what is best for us. Please give me what I really need. Amen.

What happened next?

24 Aug

Do you know the expression, "He got more than he bargained for"? This story is a bit like that. A lame man asked for money, but he was given much more!

If you didn't do yesterday's Snapshot, look at it now, because today is the second half of the story.

Read Acts 3:7–10.

Can you sit on the floor and stretch your legs out in front of you?

Can you do what the man did in verse 8, in that order?

I wonder if he'd thought that morning that he would ever walk.

Is there something you think is hopeless? Talk to God about it. Pray that things will be the way God wants.

It wasn't me!

25 Aug

Sometimes people say "It wasn't me!" when they think they might be in trouble. But Peter said that for a different reason...

Read Acts 3:11–13,16.

Peter wanted to make sure that everyone understood why the lame man was able to walk. Whose power healed the lame man? Tick the right box.

☐ Peter ☐ John ☐ Jesus

To find out the right answer, shade all the shapes with a dot.

Walk around while you say this: Thank you, God, because it was your amazing power that made the lame man walk. Please help me to remember how powerful you are, especially when

______________. Amen.

Turn around!

26 Aug

Have you ever gone the wrong way and had to turn and go back? That's what God wants us to do about our sins – turn away from them and follow his way.

Read Acts 3:17–20.

Peter told everyone:

Turn to God! Give up your sins and you will be forgiven. (Acts 3:19, CEV)

Memorise these words and actions.

Turn to God:

Turn round and then point upwards.

Give up your sins:

Pretend to push something away.

And you will be forgiven:

Make your arms into the shape of a cross.

Thank you, God, that Jesus died on the cross so that we could be forgiven. Amen.

Go to jail!

27 Aug

If you play Monopoly, you can end up in jail, but of course it's only a game. Peter and John went to jail, but it was for real. Find out why.

Read Acts 4:1–4.

What do you think is the most interesting part of this reading? Draw or write about it in the space.

Dear God, thank you for helping Peter and John be brave and share about Jesus. Please help me not to be afraid to say that I believe in you, especially when

____

Amen.

Power!

28 Aug

Clench your fists and flex your muscles so that you look really powerful. Do you think you could heal a lame man?

The Jewish leaders wanted to know how Peter and John had the power to heal the lame man. Of course, it wasn't their power. So whose power was it?

Read Acts 4:5–10.

Now write what Peter told them.

In this space, write or draw some things that are very powerful:

Thank God that his power is greater than all these things.

Only Jesus

29 Aug

Finish this drawing to show what can save this person who has jumped out of an aeroplane.

It would be strange if that person didn't want to use the only thing that could save him!

Read Acts 4:11–12.

These verses are quite difficult, but they tell us that the Jewish leaders didn't understand how important Jesus was. Some people don't want to know about Jesus (just like builders who reject certain bricks), even though he is the only person who can save them.

Other people are really glad to accept Jesus. Which are you?

Dear God, thank you that you loved me so much, you let Jesus die on the cross to save me. Amen.

Does it show?

30 Aug

If you have a school uniform, it shows everyone that you belong to a certain school. How do you think people know if someone belongs to Jesus?

Read Acts 4:13–17.

How did the Jewish leaders know that Peter and John had been with Jesus?

- ☐ Tick the right boxes.
- ☐ They wore sandals.
- ☐ They were brave.
- ☐ They healed a lame man.
- ☐ They had long hair.
- ☐ They couldn't stop speaking about Jesus.

What could you do and say to show people that you know Jesus?

Ask God to help you to be brave and speak about Jesus.

The Jewish leaders decided to tell Peter and John not to talk about Jesus.

What do you think they'll do? Find out tomorrow!

☐

You can't stop it!

31 Aug

Have you ever tried to stop a ball rolling down a hill? Imagine trying to stop an avalanche!

Read Acts 4:18–22.

Look in a mirror.

Pretend to be one of the Jewish leaders. You are cross. Wag your finger and tell Peter and John to stop talking about Jesus.

Now pretend to be Peter. Tell the Jewish leaders you must obey God, and you can't stop talking about Jesus!

Be a Jewish leader again. This time you are very cross! Warn Peter and John to stop, and then set them free.

Thank you, God, that the news about Jesus never stops spreading. Amen.

☐

Make us bold!

1 Sept

What does it mean to be bold? The four letters of the word "bold" help us to understand:

Brave

Obedient

Loving

Disciples

Read Acts 4:23–30.

Jesus' followers (the disciples) remembered that in the past lots of people had tried to stop God working. So they asked God to make them BOLD so they could keep spreading the good news about Jesus.

You could use the words the disciples prayed to ask God to help you to be BOLD too. Read the verse below and, if you really mean it, say "I am" instead of "We are", and "me" instead of "us":

"We are your servants. So make us brave enough to speak your message" (Acts 4:29, CEV).

Answered prayer

2 Sept

Sometimes we are surprised when God answers prayer – we shouldn't be!

Read Acts 4:31.

Check back to verse 29 to find out what the disciples prayed for.

What happened straight away?

____

What was everyone filled with?

____

What did everyone do?

____

It's awesome when God answers our prayers quickly, but sometimes he may want us to wait. At other times the answer might be "No". Often we don't know why, but we do know that God always knows best.

What have you learnt about God today, and from the last few days' Snapshots? Have a think and then talk to him about it.

Sharing and caring

3 Sept

It's great when people care for us, isn't it? But how easy is it to care for other people?

Read Acts 4:32–35.

God's power helped Jesus' followers to care for each other and share everything. Think of ways to care for others and share with them. Draw or list them here:

Please, God, help me to care for other people and share what I have to help them. Give me good ideas about the best ways to care. Amen.

The Bible songbook

4 Sept

All about me (Fill in the details.)

Favourite colour: ______________

Shoe size: ______________

School: ______________

Eye colour: ______________

I like thinking about:

____

My favourite song:

____

Did you know that the longest book in the Bible is a collection of songs? There are 150, and they are called psalms. Psalms are songs about God, or songs that people sing to God – a bit like hymns.

Read Psalm 139:1–6.

God knows everything you wrote under "All about me!" In fact, he knows more about you than you do! Write, "God knows" above "all about me" to complete the sentence.

Talk to God without speaking – just say the words in your head. God knows what you're thinking!

Get lost! No way!

5 Sept

When you were younger, did you ever get lost somewhere, perhaps on a beach or in a shopping centre, and nobody could find you? There's nowhere you can go where God can't find you!

Read Psalm 139:7–12.

You can't hide from God!

Draw a face to show how that makes you feel. You can copy one of these, or draw your own.

The good thing is that we'd be crazy to try and get away from God because being with him is the safest place there is.

Thank you, Father God, that wherever I go, you are there to lead and guide me. Amen.

He's always known us

6 Sept

Draw a snapshot of yourself in ten years' time.

What will you look like? What will you be doing?

Read Psalm 139:13–16.

Of course, we can only guess what we'll be doing ten years from now, but God already knows. Find the words that tell us that he knows every day of your life.

God knew even before you were born!

Thank you, Father God, that you made me. You knew everything about me, even before I was born. I praise you because of the wonderful way you created me. Amen.

I don't understand!

7 Sept

Do you know any dogs that can do algebra? Or can ride a bike? God made dogs different from humans. Humans are the most special creatures that God made.

But God made humans different from him. We are nowhere near as special as God.

Read Psalm 139:17–18.

Trying to understand God is a bit like a dog trying to understand us – we can understand a bit, but not everything. It's impossible to understand God, because God is much greater than we are.

Is there something about God that you don't understand? Tell God, but ask him to help you to trust him anyway. Then praise God because he is so much greater than we are.

Tell it like it is

8 Sept

Circle the words you might expect to hear in a prayer.

KILL FORGIVE HATE
HOLY ENEMIES

See how many of these words you can find in today's passage:

Read Psalm 139:19–22.

Did this prayer surprise you? Do you think the person should have said this to God?

Remember what we found out at the weekend? We can't hide our feelings from God – so we might as well be honest when we talk to him. We shouldn't hate people, but if we do, it's better to admit it to God and ask him to help us.

Is something or someone troubling you? Tell God how you really feel about it.

What are you thinking?

9 Sept

Colour the shapes with dots to see what is hidden.

Imagine if the people you live with knew your hidden thoughts. Would you like that?

We know that God knows our thoughts. Find out what the writer thought about that in the next part of the psalm.

Read Psalm 139:23–24.

It's good that God knows our thoughts – even our bad ones. Not because he wants to punish us, but because he wants to help us to be better people.

Say the words of Psalm 139:23–24 out loud, as your own prayer to God.

God knows me

10 Sept

Dave Godfrey writes:

When I became a Christian I was a teenager. I really wanted to know what God thought of me. I didn't think I was very important to God.

I remember reading Psalm 139 in my Bible. It is an amazing psalm written by King David and it totally blew me away! It says that God "created every part of me" and that all he did "is strange and wonderful".
(Check out verses 13 and 14.)

David says, "You have looked deep into my heart, Lord, and know all about me."

God does know me and loves me! He knows my thoughts, my actions and my words, even before I speak them!

When I read those words, I changed the way I thought about myself – I began to realise just how important I was to God!

The great thing is that he thinks about you in exactly the same way!

Supper time

11 Sept

Some people say that the death of Jesus was a big mistake. It wasn't. God had planned it and Jesus knew what was going to happen. On the night before he died Jesus explained it all to his friends. Would they understand?

Read John 13:1–3.

Find three things that Jesus knew:

1 ______________________________

2 ______________________________

3 ______________________________

Jesus knew what was going to happen to him and yet he still went through it all – for us.

Who else was making plans (verse 2)? Did they work?

Imagine you're one of Jesus' friends. Tell Jesus what you feel: about hearing his plans; when you see him dying on the cross; when you've seen him alive again.

☐

Don't wash me!

12 Sept

What's the nastiest job you can think of? Imagine the richest person in the world doing it!

Read John 13:4–5.

Draw the correct picture in the white boxes:

Jesus tied a ☐ round his waist.

He poured ☐ into a ☐.

Then he washed the disciples' ☐.

Peter was shocked! Jesus was doing a slave's job, not behaving like a leader. Peter didn't understand.

Find another person and read verses 6–9 together in parts.

Now Peter understood. Unless Jesus made him clean he couldn't belong to Jesus. Neither can we.

Next time you have a bath or shower imagine Jesus washing away all the bad things inside you.

☐

Do what I do

13 Sept

Did you ever play "Follow my leader" where you all copy the person at the front?

How can we follow Jesus?

Read John 13:12–15.

Jesus wanted his friends to do what he did, serving others.

Ask Jesus to help you understand that following him means behaving the way he did, even if we don't feel like it.

Does your way of serving others look like Jesus' way?

Invite your mum/dad/carer/church leaders to a foot-washing party. Give them a nice soapy foot massage in warm water, dry their feet well and put their shoes back on.

Just for fun!

Who is it?

14 Sept

How do you feel when your good friend doesn't act like your friend?

Read John 13:21–30.

Jesus knew that one of his friends was about to betray him. Imagine how he felt.

Jesus understands how we feel because he's felt those feelings too.

Even though Jesus knew, the disciples couldn't work out who the betrayer was. Fit the words into the grid to help them out.

BREAD JESUS TROUBLES
SATAN BETRAY

				↓				
■	■	■	■		E			
■							E	
		E			■	■	■	■
	E					■	■	■
■	■	■	■		A			

When Judas went out, Jesus knew that horrible things were about to happen. Talk with Jesus about horrible things happening in the world today.

Bad or good?

15 Sept

When Judas betrayed Jesus, was it good or bad? When Jesus died on the cross, was it good or bad? Why do we call it Good Friday? If you're not sure, ask someone.

Read John 13:31–32.

Although he was going to die a horrible death, Jesus knew why he was dying and what would happen afterwards.

Colour yellow all the squares that have a dot.

G·	L	O	R	Y
E	L·	W	I	N
R	W	O·	W	N
F	A	B	R·	X
B	R	I	L	Y·

Write the word here:

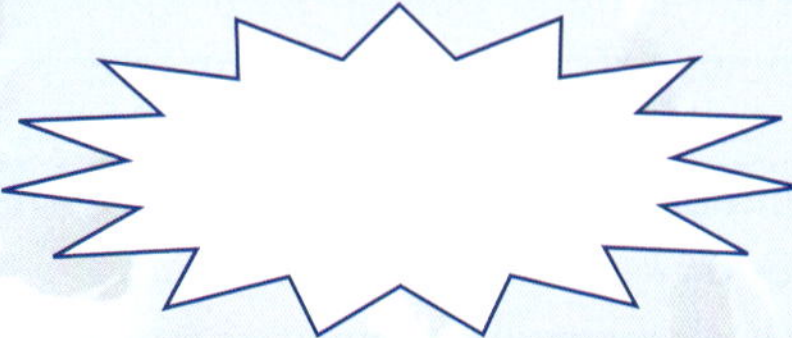

Glory means a sign of God's greatness and splendour. How did Jesus' death show this?

Jesus, you're wonderful,
You died for me,
Showing God's glory
For all to see.

A new command

16 Sept

How do people know which school you go to? Do you have a uniform or school badge?

Read John 13:34–35.

Jesus gave his disciples a really important new rule (or commandment). What was it?

Starting at the L, write down every other letter.

LGOTVHEQEJAMCRHPODTEHNEMRP

_ _ _ _ / _ _ _ _ / _ _ _ _ _

People who see your school badge or uniform know which school you belong to. What will everyone know if you love each other? (Read it backwards.)

SELPICSID 'SUSEJ ERA UOY ←

_ _ _/ _ _ _ /_ _ _ _ _ _ /

_ _ _ _ _ _ _ _ _ _

The badge of a disciple is LOVE.

If you want to be Jesus' disciple, ask him to help you keep his new command.

Living God's way

17 Sept

Today's Bible passage is written here. It's from **1 Peter 1:13–16.**

"Be alert and think straight. Put all your hope in how kind God will be to you when Jesus Christ appears. Behave like obedient children. Don't let your lives be controlled by your desires, as they used to be. Always live as God's holy people should, because God is the one who chose you, and he is holy. That's why the Scriptures say, 'I am the holy God, and you must be holy too.'"

Put a bold line under the things Peter says people should do. Put a dotted line under what people shouldn't do. Put a circle around the word "holy".

"Holy" means something or someone who is unspoilt and set apart from normal things. God is completely holy. There is no bad in him at all.

Can you put how God wants us to live in your own words?

Are you worried?

18 Sept

Do you ever worry about things and not know who to talk to? Peter understood all about that!

Read 1 Peter 5:6–7.

Use Codebreaker 4 on page 96 to work out what Peter's advice is.

Even though God is great and powerful, he still cares for you.

Imagine yourself going to sit with God. Tell him about anything that's worrying you at the moment in the news, at school, in your family or something no one else knows about.

What do you know about God that shows you can trust him with anything?

Be alert!

19 Sept

Have you ever been "on" in a game where everyone else has to get back to base without you catching them? You need to watch really carefully. Life is like that sometimes.

Read 1 Peter 5:8–11.

Why do you need to carefully watch? (verse 8)

____

What's the best way to stop the devil attacking? (verse 9)

____

____

How will God help you resist? (verse 10)

____

God is more powerful than anything or anyone – he will always help you if you ask him.

Dear God, sometimes it's really hard not to do wrong things, especially __________________

____________________________.

Please make my faith strong and firm so that I can resist temptation.

How holy are you?

20 Sept

(No, not holey like the picture!!)

In his letter that we've just read, Peter talks about being holy. In fact, loads of the Bible is about being holy. We know that God is holy, but why would you want to be holy? Because Jesus said that's how we have to be.

In **Matthew 5:48** Jesus says we have to be like God – that's holy and perfect.

The goal of Christians is HOLINESS. Jesus is our hero and we're trying to be like him.

At least we'll always have something to work at, so we should never be bored.

And the good news is that as we let Jesus live out his life through us, we start to become holy because Jesus is holy.

Don't mess with God!

21 Sept

Messages are important. God had a message for his people. It was serious stuff! Read on to find out more...

Read Amos 2:4–6.

Amos was a shepherd, but then God asked him to give a warning message to people who were not living in a way that pleased God.

What was the message for God's people in Judah (in the south) and God's people in Israel (in the north)? Fill in the blanks.

The Lord says:

I w_ _l p _ n _ _ _ t _ _ m.

What had the people of Judah and Israel done wrong? Check out verses 4 and 6 again. (Fill in these blanks too.)

R _ j _ _ _ G _ _ 's

t_ _ch _ _ _ _

R _ f_ _ e t_ o _ _ _ _

W _ rsh_ pp _ _ f_ _ s _ g_ds

Dear God, help me to please you today, especially when I'm

_______________.

Serious stuff

22 Sept

Have you ever had to miss out on something, stay in at playtime, or lose your pocket money? Punishments aren't meant to be fun. What are they for?

Read Amos 3:1–2.

Can you put God's message in your own words?

True or false? (Answers on page 192.)

God expected his people to obey his laws. T/F

God's people could do whatever they liked and it didn't matter. T/F

God's people had to be punished because they had sinned. T/F

God stopped loving his people because they disobeyed him. T/F

God never stops loving us either.

Go to a place where it doesn't matter if you make a noise. Shout out three times: "God will never stop loving me!"

Stop!

23 Sept

How many road signs can you think of? Draw one here.

Some road signs tell you to stop or go a different way.

Read Amos 5:6–9.

What did Amos tell God's people to do?

Use Codebreaker 4 on page 96 to crack the code.

✳✵✲❀ ✢✡✣✫ ✳✮

✳★✥ ✬✮✲✤ ✡❀✤

✹✮✵ ✷☆✬✬ ✬☆✶✥

____

____

____

What do verses 8 and 9 remind you of? Genesis 1:4,6,14 will give you a clue.

Talk with God and ask him to forgive you now. Even though he is so great, he will forgive you. Thank him for that.

Bad news, good advice

24 Sept

If someone gets into trouble at school, do you hear people whispering, "What did they do?"

Read Amos 5:10–15.

The people had done many terrible things. Which three things are mentioned in verse 12?

1__________________________

2__________________________

3__________________________

Use a pen to draw a big cross through the bad news above.

Verse 15 contains some good advice. Put these words in the right order to find out what it is:

hate love what what is is evil right

Now put a big tick beside the good advice above. Can you learn those words?

Think of one evil thing you can hate. Think of one good thing you can love. Ask an adult you trust to help you if you get stuck.

No kidding!

25 Sept

It's no good saying or doing something unless we really mean it – no kidding!

Read Amos 5:23–24.

We mustn't pretend to do, say or sing what God wants, as some of his people had been doing.

Look at verse 24 again. 'Justice' means doing what is right and fair. 'Righteousness' (called 'fairness' in some Bibles) means having goodness that comes from God.

What does God want us to do?

Let justice and righteousness flow in our lives like...

a lake   a stream

a reservoir   a puddle

a pond   a river

Close your eyes and imagine you are a fast-moving stream, bringing goodness and justice wherever you go. Would you be wide or narrow? Noisy or swiftly silent? Just tell God what thoughts come into your mind.

One day...

26 Sept

When someone you trust makes a promise, you may have to wait a while before it comes true, but you know that it will happen one day! Today we read about a promise God made to his people...

Read Amos 9:13–15.

Can you finish off these pictures?

What does God's message say about these?

Some of God's promises have already come true. The rest will come true when God's people live with him in heaven for ever. Thank God that his promises always come true.

Make a dove

27 Sept

A dove is a symbol of peace. Take a sticky note and fold it in half so the sticky edge sticks to itself. Then draw the outline of a dove and cut it out. Now you have a dove!

Keep it in your pocket, or pencil case, to remind you to be a peacemaker today.

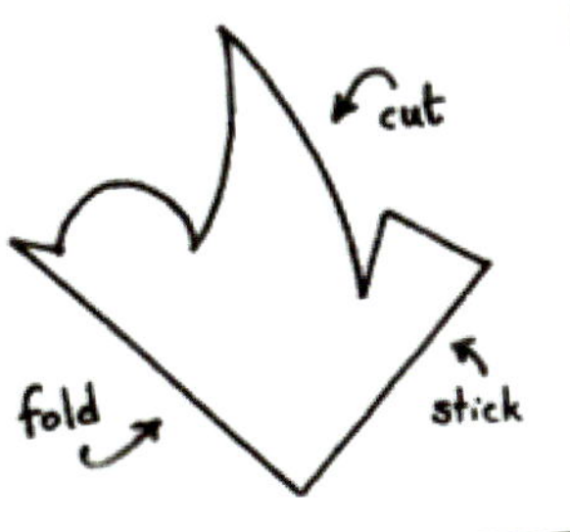

New, not old!

28 Sept

Try to put four old socks on one foot on top of each other.

How hard was that to do? Now take all the socks off and put just one new sock on! That is much easier – to replace lots of old socks with one clean smart sock! Find out about getting rid of something old and starting again with something new.

Read Ephesians 4:22–24.

Cross out the wrong answers:

If we get rid of our old bike/clothes/life, we can put on our new hat/life/shoes.

Our hearts and minds must be completely orange/new/plastic.

Put the right words in the gaps:

sorry forgive new

If we are really _ _ _ _ _ for the wrong things in our old life, God will _ _ _ _ _ _ _ _ us and give us a _ _ _ life. Then he will help us to become more like him.

How does that make you feel? Talk to God about it now.

Jokes page

How can you tell which end of a worm is which?

Tickle it in the middle and see which end laughs!

What do you call a man with a wig on his head?

Aaron

What did the two lights say to each other?

Let's go out together.

Why was 6 afraid of 7?

Because 7,8,9!

What is the most intelligent mountain?

Mount Cleverest.

What did the mayonnaise say to the fridge?

"Please close the door, I'm dressing."

Important information!

29 Sept

If you learn a musical instrument, play in a sports team, or join a swimming club, it's important to know how to begin and how to keep going!

There are usually some "Dos and Don'ts" to learn...

In today's passage there are some "Dos and Don'ts" for living life God's way.

Read Ephesians 4:25–32.

Can you put the right verse numbers beside these?

Don't tell lies
Do tell the truth
Verse: ______________________

Don't use harmful words
Do use helpful words
Verse: ______________________

Don't shout at people
Do be kind
Verse: ______________________

Decide which one of the "Do" list you need to do more. Underline it, then ask God to help you to do it.

☐

Copycat!

30 Sept

A good way to learn something new is to watch someone else doing it and then have a go ourselves. Remember the game "Follow the leader"?

That's how we follow Jesus. He's shown us the very best way to live and he helps us to be like him!

Read Ephesians 5:1–2.

Imagine that there is someone in your class who is left out.

Other people are unkind to them and they seem sad and lonely.

What would Jesus do if he came to your school?

So what could you do if you want to be like Jesus?

Talk with God about a way in which you could be like Jesus when you are at school.

☐

Switch the light on!

1 Oct

Have you ever stumbled around in the dark? What a difference when the light's on and you can see clearly!

Read Ephesians 5:8–11.

Question: How can we live like people who belong to the light, not darkness?

Answer: Join up the words from verse 10 in order.

Try	**learn**	**Lord**
to	**what**	
pleases	**the**	

When is it difficult to please the Lord? Is it when you are at home, at school or when you are with your friends? Think about it and then say this prayer:

Please God, help me to keep away from things that belong to the darkness. Help me to live like someone who belongs to the light, especially when I'm ___________

____

Amen.

More good advice!

2 Oct

Do you remember the good advice from Amos on 24 September?

Read Ephesians 5:15–17.

Here's some more advice for living as people who belong to the light, not darkness. Write "YES!" or "NO!" beside each statement, then check page 192 for the answers.

It doesn't matter how you live. _____

Be careful how you live. _______

Make good use of every opportunity. ________

Worry about opportunities later. ______

Do what you think is best. ______

Find out what the Lord wants you to do. ____

Ask God to help you to hate what is evil and love what is right, so you can live in a way which pleases him.

Thanks God!

3 Oct

Think about these questions and write your answers across the faces.

What's been fun in the past few days?

What's been hard but you've survived?

Has God been with you in both situations?

Read Ephesians 5:20.

What should we give thanks for?

Circle the right answer:

Nothing/One or two things/

Everything!

Look at the three faces. You can be thankful to God for the things you wrote down. What else can you thank God for?

Talk with him now.

Who's who?

4 Oct

Do you know any old people? In today's Bible verses we are going to find out about two old people and a king!

Read Luke 1:5–7.

Join the right name label to each person.

Elizabeth, Herod, Zechariah

The Bible tells us something special about Zechariah and Elizabeth in Luke 1:6. Does that remind you of anyone?

Check out Genesis 6:8–9 and Genesis 7:5.

What are the names of the old people you thought about earlier? Thank God for them and ask that they will live lives that please God.

Meet John!

5 Oct

What kind of baby were you when you were tiny?

Sleepy
Happy
Hungry
Active
Noisy
Smelly

Read Luke 1:8–17.

What did the angel say about Zechariah's baby? Underline in red what John will be like. Underline in green how he will help people get ready for the Lord.

15 Your son will be a great servant of the Lord. He must never drink wine or beer, and the power of the Holy Spirit will be with him from the time
he is born. **16** John will lead many
people in Israel to turn back to the
Lord their God. **17** He will go ahead
of the Lord with the same power and spirit that Elijah had. And because of John, parents will be more thoughtful of their children. And people who now disobey God will begin to think as they ought to. That is how John will get people ready for the Lord.

God had promised to rescue his people and John was part of that plan. Thank God that he keeps his promises.

God does it again!

6 Oct

Can you remember what God had told Zechariah?

God can do anything, but Zechariah wasn't too sure...

Read Luke 1:18–20.

Why wasn't Zechariah sure about the news the angel gave him?
Because

____

____________________________.

What did the angel say would happen because Zechariah didn't believe God's message?
He would be unable to

____

____________________________.

Thank you, God, for your power. Please help me to remember that you can do the impossible. Help me to trust you at all times, especially when

____

____

____________________________.

God means it

7 Oct

Sometimes, someone says something to you, but you know they don't really mean it. God is not like that!

Read Luke 1:21–25.

God had told Zechariah important things.

Fill in the missing words.
Tick the promise if it happened.
Put a cross if it didn't.

What did the angel promise would happen to Elizabeth?

☐ She would have a _ _ _ _ even though she was very _ _ _.

How did the people know something amazing had happened to Zechariah?

☐ Because he could not _ _ _ _ _.

God always means what he says! Tell him how that makes you feel.

Name the baby

8 Oct

Sometimes it's hard to think of a name for a new baby. But God had already told Zechariah and Elizabeth what they should call their son so they didn't have that problem. What happened?

Read Luke 1:59–66.

Write Zechariah's words on the writing tablet. (A writing tablet is another name for a message board!)

Why did Zechariah write it down? He could/couldn't speak. What happened next? He could/couldn't speak.

What plans do you think God has for your life? Ask an adult you trust to help you answer this.

Thank you, God, that you had great plans for John and you have great plans for me, too.

More about John

9 Oct

Have you ever been given a message that you had to pass on to someone else? That's what Zechariah did. God gave him a message about John to tell everyone, so he did!

Read Luke 1:76–80.

Can you tick the right boxes?

God had a special job for:

☐ John ☐ Jack ☐ James

He would be a:

☐ painter ☐ postman ☐ prophet

That meant he would:

☐ keep quiet ☐ speak God's messages
☐ write a book

John would tell people to:

☐ get ready for Jesus
☐ have a holiday ☐ work harder

Think of someone, "God's messenger", who tells you God's messages. Why not text or write to thank the person who brings you God's messages?

☐

No longer a baby

10 Oct

What do you want to be when you grow up? Have your ideas changed since you were younger?

God told Zechariah what John would be when he grew up, and remember, God always means what he says.

Read Luke 3:2–6.

What was John telling everyone to do? Start at the letter 'T'. Go along the row twice, and write down every other letter in the spaces:

Tmuyronuarwsaiynfsr!o

_ _ _ _ / _ _ _ _ / _ _ _ _
_ _ _ _ _ _ _ _ .

Sin is when we don't live the way God wants. Think about any sins that you need to turn away from. Talk to God about them now. You can tell him you are sorry, and ask him to forgive you.

☐

Fact file: Luke

11 Oct

Who? Luke was a Gentile (non-Jew) doctor and writer. He was a friend of Paul and travelled with him on some of his mission journeys.

What? He wrote down stories about Jesus (Luke's Gospel) and the sequel, the Acts of the Apostles.

When? We don't know exactly when Luke lived, but it was during the 1st century. He probably wrote the Gospel and Acts around 60–70 AD.

Why? Luke made a "careful study" of stories about Jesus and then wrote them down for his friend Theophilus. After Jesus went back to heaven Luke continued the story with the Acts of the Apostles, telling how people spread the good news about Jesus.

Main point? The most important thing Luke wanted people to know was that Jesus is the Saviour of the world.

☐

Grumbling

12 Oct

God's people had been kept as slaves in Egypt, with not much food. They escaped to the desert, but they still didn't have much food!

Read Exodus 16:1–5.

Are these statements true (T) or false (F)?

(Answers on page 192.)

The people complained to God. T/F

The people thought they had eaten lots of food in Egypt. T/F

God promised that food would pop up out of the ground. T/F

God's people were so busy grumbling about their rumbling tummies, they forgot about everything that God had done for them.

Dear God, I'm sorry that I grumble about ________________. Thank you for all you have done for me, especially ____________. Help me to remember this when I feel like grumbling.

☐

God and grumbles

13 Oct

Ever been in a group of people who were all complaining about the same thing – like school dinners, the rain, or a late bus? It's easy to join in, isn't it?

Read Exodus 16:6–12.

What did God's people see in the morning? (verse 10)

____

What were they going to eat in the evening?

____

What were they going to eat in the morning?

____

God's people would discover that God had heard their grumbles and was doing something about it. But do you think God was pleased that they had grumbled?

Thank God that he still loves us and cares for us, even when we grumble. Ask him to help you not to grumble.

Food, glorious food!

14 Oct

You can have food delivered to your house – have a pizza sent round, or order a Chinese meal. But have you ever seen food delivered the way God sent food to his people?

Read Exodus 16:13–15.

So how did this special food arrive each day? Unjumble the words to find out.

Each evening aulqsi _______ flew into the camp. Every morning there were hnit lafkes__________ __________on the ground.

What did the people ask when they saw this?

God provided tema __________ and rebad ______________ for everyone!

Thank you, God, that you provided the Israelites with the food they needed. Thank you for the food I eat, especially ______________ and ______________. Amen.

Listen carefully!

15 Oct

What happens if you don't listen carefully to instructions? Find out what happened to some of God's people.

Read Exodus 16:16–20.

How much food were the people told to gather each day?

____

Did they have enough each day? **Y/N**

What were they told not to do?

____

Did everyone obey? **Y/N**

Write or draw what happened to the food that they tried to save:

Please, God, help us to remember that you always know what is best for us. Help us to follow your instructions in the Bible and to live your way. Amen.

Have a rest!

16 Oct

Why do you think people like weekends?

Read Exodus 16:21–30.

Cross out the wrong words:

On the first/sixth day the people gathered less/twice as much.

God told them: "Tomorrow is the holy Sabbath, a day of work/rest to remember/forget me so there will be no /lots more food on the ground."

For many people, the Sabbath (or Sunday) is a day kept special for God when they don't have to work and they can relax. It was all God's idea in the first place!

Check out Genesis 2:2–3.

Stretch out on your back and relax. Thank God for rest days and ask him to help you make each Sunday a special day to think about him.

Funky food

17 Oct

Funky food 1: Manna

God put it on the sand every morning for the Israelites to pick up. It was called manna because it sounds like the Hebrew for "What is it?" It was like small flakes (no, not cornflakes!), whitish in colour and tasted a bit like honey. It was cooked and made into special manna bread.

Funky food 2: Quail

Quail are small game birds, about the size of a football. When they came, they were everywhere and were easy enough for the Israelites to catch.

God provided this food for his people to show how much he cared for them. God's people ate manna and quail every day for 40 years in the desert (Exodus 16:13–35).

Psst! In many parts of the world people eat the same food every day. It is only in the western world that we have such a varied diet!

Holy rules

18 Oct

The Israelites got very fed up in the desert and stopped acting like they were God's people. God decided to give them some holy rules that would teach them to live the way he wanted them to. That would make them holy.

Read Leviticus 19:1–4.

In the word puzzle find these words that God used: rules, holy, must, respect, Sabbath, father, mother, idols, abandon.

Starting from the arrow, use the leftover letters to discover why God wanted his people to obey his rules.

_ AM _ _ _ _ _ _ _ _

R	E	H	T	O	M	I	A
E	H	T	I	D	O	L	S
S	F	A	T	H	E	R	O
P	A	B	A	N	D	O	N
E	L	B	S	E	L	U	R
C	Y	A	G	H	O	L	Y
T	O	S	M	U	S	T	D

Say "thank you" to God because he shows us how to be holy.

More about food

19 Oct

God has said people should do certain things to show that they love and obey him. At one time God asked people to give offerings of food. He asks us to do different things to show we love him.

Read Leviticus 19:5–10.

After all the rules about food, God says something about the grapes and grain that have fallen. Why does he say that? What does this show us about God?

Make a list of the things you could offer to God which would help people who have less than you. If we help others we are being like God, we are being holy.

Offer some time to God in silence and listen to what he might say to you.

God rules!

20 Oct

The Bible is not full of "Do nots" that stop us living. It is a book that gives us new life!

Read Leviticus 19:11–18.

What does God keep saying about himself?

'I am ___ ____ _______ _____.'

These rules all have an important message.

What do they say about God?

What do they say about how we should live with other people?

On the notice board write down two holy rules you think should be kept – one about God and one about other people.

1____________________

2____________________

God wants us to be happy and so gives us good rules to live by.

Tell God all the things he has helped you to be good at, or given you to make life better.

My Shepherd

21 Oct

King David wrote this song. When he was young, David was a shepherd. It was tough looking after his sheep. He even had to fight bears and lions!

When he was older, a powerful enemy tried to kill David. He had to run away and hide in the hills. When he was in danger, David must have thought of things he needed. What does he say in this psalm?

Read Psalm 23:1.

Draw David hiding in the picture. In what ways was God like a shepherd to David?

Thank you, God that you are always looking after me, even when things seem tough.

You let me rest

22 Oct

Have you ever been hot and tired but had to keep going? Sometimes David's enemies hunted him day and night. He had to keep going across bare rocks. It was freezing at night and baking hot by day.

Read Psalm 23:2.

What were the fields of grass for?____________________

What were the streams like?____________________

God knew what David needed and he knows what you need too.

Sit quietly and thank God for the way he looks after you.

You lead me

23 Oct

Have you ever followed a path that led nowhere? Sometimes sheep will follow a path that leads right over a cliff!

For David, following the right path was sometimes a matter of life or death.

Read Psalm 23:3.

Put a circle around the shepherd whose path leads away from danger.

Following God always leads to the right place!

Unscramble these words from verse 3.

"Oyu elda em galon het grith pasht."

Write them along the path and say them as a prayer.

I won't be afraid

24 Oct

When you're afraid, what do you do? Whistle a happy tune? Hide away somewhere? Pretend nothing is wrong?

Read Psalm 23:4.

David said that even if he walked through ______________________ he wouldn't be afraid because

______________________________.

Draw yourself walking beside the shepherd. In pencil, write on the hillside things that frighten you. God is more powerful than anyone or anything else.

Rub out the scary words and as each one disappears, thank God that he looks after you.

Celebrate

25 Oct

Someone in your class is having a big party. Loads of invitations are given out. But you don't get one. How do you feel?

Read Psalm 23:5–6.

God always wants to celebrate with him! He never leaves us out!

Imagine God laying the table for a great feast.

Imagine him helping you to sit down at the table.

Imagine him serving your favourite food.

Imagine him bringing you second and third helpings.

Imagine him checking that you have enough to drink.

What will you say to him now? Use verse 6 as your prayer.

Muddled up!

26 Oct

We've muddled up a great bit from one of the psalms. Can you work out what verse it is and which psalm it is from? (Two dots stand for one space!)

e..his

le!...P

s..our

Ord...i

we..ar

..and..

..God,

95:7

salm..

..peop

The...L

Have you ever had a go at writing a psalm? Check out page 168 to find out what happened to Jenny when she had a go!

Temptations

27 Oct

A temptation is when we think about doing something that is wrong, an unholy act. Sometimes this idea can just appear in our heads and it can be hard to ignore. Where do these thoughts come from?

Read James 1:12–15.

True or false:

Temptation is God's fault. T/F

God doesn't use evil to tempt us. T/F

Our desires tempt us to sin. T/F

BUT, if we are strong and ignore the temptations we feel then God will reward us with life that lasts for ever.

Ask God to make you strong and able to ignore the temptations you may have.

How can you stay faithful to God when you are being tempted to do or say bad things?

Holy listening

28 Oct

James' letter is a set of instructions to help God's people all over the world. James wants people not only to love God but to show that they love him by doing holy things. Hold one ear and...

Read James 1:19–25.

What does James say about listening and doing?

If we listen to God what kind of person will that make us?

Find a mirror and have a good look at your face. Notice your teeth, the shape of your eyebrows and any marks on your skin. Turn away. Have you forgotten what you look like already? That would be silly. And it would be silly to hear what God wants but not do it!

Can you think of a time when you heard what you were meant to do but disobeyed?

Obeying God's holy requests can be difficult. Tell God you are sorry for the times you don't listen to what he says.

Everyone's equal

29 Oct

Everyone in the world looks different. How many differences can you think of? Some people are treated badly because of the way they look.

Read James 2:1–4.

James talks about two people coming to a church meeting. What's the difference between them?

What would be the wrong way to behave towards them? (verse 3)

Prejudice means that we treat someone unfairly because we don't like something about them. Prejudices have led to wars and suffering.

What would be the right way to treat the two men?

Is there anyone in your class at school who is treated badly because they are different?

Ask God to help you to treat them fairly.

Holy doings

30 Oct

James has already said that we need to listen to and obey God. He goes further and tells us what should happen when we have faith in God.

Read James 2:14–18.

Is it OK to have faith in God but not do anything to show that it matters and makes a difference?

Can you think of a situation in your life like the one in verses 15 and 16?

Pick one practical thing that you think God would like you to do today which will show that believing in God and living his way makes a difference. It might be doing something to help at home or being kind to someone at school.

Actions take courage.

Dear God, make me brave, strong, determined and kind so that I work for you and make a difference in someone's life.

Holy wisdom

31 Oct

Being wise isn't about being clever, it's about knowing what God wants and doing it.

Read James 3:13–18.

Are there things that you feel jealous or selfish about? Are there times when you don't bring peace or gentleness or friendliness? Write these down on scraps of paper.

As you ask God to help you to be less like this, tear the scraps of paper up into small pieces and throw them away. Be holy in how you think and in what you do!

How does James describe God's wisdom, the wisdom from above? (verse 17) Write them here to help you remember.

That's how to behave wisely!

Humble and holy!

1 Nov

Being humble means that we know we will never be as holy as God. But God knows that and he still loves us. Being friends with God means we can be honest with him.

Read James 4:7–10.

What does James tell people to do to help them come closer to God? How many different things can you count? Which ones do you find most surprising?

It might seem strange for us to be sad to get closer to God. God wants us to tell him everything. As we do, we become aware of his goodness and our own failures. We should share all our feelings with God, the sad and happy ones, the good and bad ones.

Find a quiet space where you can be alone with God. Share all the feelings you have with him and know that he is close to you.

Bad flu!

2 Nov

Callum writes:

One day I started a cold which just got worse and worse. I lay in bed feeling really grotty. Then I felt this urge to go downstairs and pray with my mum. We prayed that she'd make the right choice about whether to take me to the doctor or not. I was really scared.

In the end we went to the doctor who said I just had very bad flu. After five more visits to the doctor, mum said she wanted me to go to the hospital for a check-up. It was a good thing we did. When we got there, they found out that I had pneumonia! I couldn't believe it!

Lots of people prayed for me and I got better really fast. I'm sure God helped my mum make the right choices in all this, and helped me get better!

Ask the doctor

3 Nov

What do you think of first when you see the word 'power'? Ask someone else what they think too. Did you think of God?

Read Matthew 8:1–4.

If you had a skin rash, what might the doctor do?

- [ ] Give you some ointment.
- [ ] Suggest you soak in a bath of salt water.
- [ ] Prescribe some medicine.

Why did the man ask Jesus for help?

Fill in the gaps with a, e, i, o or u.

J_s_s h _ d th _ p _ w _ r
t _ m_k_ p_ _pl_ w_ll

What did Jesus do for the man?

Can you make a card for someone you know who is unwell? Pray for them as you make it.

Jesus does it again

4 Nov

Let's start with some exercises! Stand up, turn around, bend your knees, have a stretch and then sit down! The paralysed man in today's story wouldn't have been able to do those things.

Read Matthew 9:1–8.

Jesus showed everyone that he had God's power. What did he do to help the paralysed man?

Unjumble the words to find out.

Faegorv ish isns Hadele mih

How would you answer Jesus' question in verse 5?

The people praised God when they saw what Jesus did. Wave your arms in the air and praise him for his power. Kneel down and thank him for his forgiveness.

Anyone can follow!

5 Nov

Taxes – money that everyone has to give the government – help pay for things like roads and public buildings. In Bible times, no one liked tax collectors, because sometimes they were dishonest and took more money than they should.

Read Matthew 9:9–13.

Did Jesus mind that Matthew was a tax collector? Y/N

Did the Jewish leaders mind that Jesus had a meal with Matthew? Y/N

What did Jesus tell them? Tick the right picture.

I didn't come to invite only good people to be my followers, I came to invite sinners.

Thank Jesus that he didn't come for good people but for those who knew they had got things wrong.

The news spreads

6 Nov

When something amazing happens, people hear about it! In today's Bible verses, two people heard about Jesus' power and went to him for help.

Read Matthew 9:18–26.

Put the words in the right spaces.
touch, well, live, hands, died, cloak

What did the Jewish official say to Jesus?

My daughter has just _ _ _ _;
but come and place your _ _ _ _ _
on her and she will _ _ _ _.

What did the woman think about Jesus?

If I only _ _ _ _ _ his _ _ _ _ _
I will get _ _ _ _.

God has power to heal people in different ways. Can you think of some others?

Thank God that he does heal. Who can you pray for who is ill at the moment?

Blind people see!

7 Nov

Sue Clutterham who writes for Snapshots, says:

"My friend, Jan, had trouble with her eyes. The doctors said she might go blind. We prayed for her and then she found out about an eye surgeon who gave her some special laser treatment. Her eyes are fine now. Praise God!" Read about two blind people that Jesus helped.

Read Matthew 9:27–31.

Number the boxes to put the story in the correct order:

- ☐ Jesus touched their eyes.
- ☐ They answered, "Yes, sir!" Jesus said:
- ☐ "Do you believe that I can heal you?"
- ☐ They could see again!
- ☐ They asked Jesus to help
- 1 Two blind men followed Jesus along the road.

Sing a song of praise to Jesus!

Talkative!

8 Nov

Are you a chatterbox? How long do you think you could last without speaking (not counting when you are asleep)?

Read Matthew 9:32–33.

The man in today's Bible verses couldn't talk at all. How would that make you feel? Draw the shape of your mouth here:

How do you think the man felt after meeting Jesus? Draw the shape of the man's mouth, then write what he might have said in the speech bubble.

Thank you, God, that you gave Jesus the power to get rid of the man's demon and to heal him so that he could speak. Amen.

Jesus cares

9 Nov

For this Snapshot, the Bible verses are here! Read them, then follow the instructions:

Read Matthew 9:35–38.

Jesus has pity on people

35 Jesus went to every town and village.
He taught in their meeting places and
preached the good news about God's
kingdom. Jesus also healed every kind of
disease and sickness. **36** When he saw
the crowds, he felt sorry for them. They
were confused and helpless, like sheep
without a shepherd. **37** He said to his
disciples, "A large crop is in the fields,
but there are only a few workers. **38** Ask
the Lord in charge of the harvest to send
out workers to bring it in."

1) In verse 35, circle the words that tell what Jesus did.

2) Underline the word in verse 6 that tells how Jesus felt when he saw the crowds.

3) Draw a box around the name of the animal that Jesus thought the people were like.

4) What did Jesus tell his disciples to do? Draw a wavy line under the words in verse 38.

Jesus cared so much for people and did so much for them. Write a letter to Jesus to thank him for loving everyone – including you!

Prayer time

10 Nov

Hands together, eyes closed

Have you been taught at school or in church to pray with your hands together and eyes closed? Putting our hands together means we won't be fiddling with something! Closing our eyes helps us concentrate on God. However, Dave Godfrey suggests some different ways to pray.

Kneeling down – shows God I am really serious about him, just like a servant would bow before a king. Writing or drawing – helps me to think carefully what I want to say to God. This could be a short letter, a paper aeroplane or a sketch.

Chatting to God all the time (out loud or in your head) – in the classroom, walking along the road, waiting for a friend.

Shouting and clapping – getting enthusiastic about God!

Singing – using someone else's words to talk to God.

Raising my hands – using our bodies to pray.

God loves it when we pray!

Rock solid

11 Nov

Look at the list below. Draw a red line under any words that could describe a rock.

solid weak doesn't change

strong dangerous protects

soft reliable always different

Read Psalm 95:1–2.

Look at the list again. Put a blue line under any words that remind you of God. Are there any words that have two lines underneath them? Why do you think that is? (Psst! The Good News Bible uses the words "protects us" instead of "rock".)

How does the psalm writer say we should come to God? Why?

Sing a song of praise to God. Can you get anyone else to sing with you?

Who's the greatest?

12 Nov

How many superheroes can you think of? What are their powers? Now compare them to God.

Read Psalm 95:3–5.

How do you know God is greater than any superhero? (verse 3)

____

Fill in the missing words to find out why God is the greatest:

He rules the whole e _ _ _ _

He made the s _ _

He _ _ _ _ _ _ _ the dry l _ _ _

God is bigger than everything in the world – after all, he made the world!

God, you're the greatest! You made the earth and the sea. You are more powerful than anything because you made everything.

You're the greatest!

God cares

13 Nov

Have you ever had a pet? How did you care for it properly?

Read Psalm 95:6–7.

Write inside this sheep some of the ways in which God looks after you.

How does verse 6 suggest we respond to all that God has done? Sometimes people bow or kneel down in worship to show that they know God is much greater than they are. Think about what you've learnt about God in Psalm 95.

Get down on your knees and use your thoughts to worship God. If you know it, sing 'Our God is a great big God!'

Jenny's psalm!

14 Nov

Psalms are songs and poems that say something about God. Have you ever tried writing one? When a girl called Jenny Conde was 10 she had a go at writing a psalm. Here's her story...

"I really wanted to say sorry to God for not following him. I also wanted to thank him for loving me so much. I had just come to realise that he made me perfect and that he loved me the way I was. I wanted to let him know that he was really special to me."

Here's what she wrote:

Lord, we're sorry for the wrong things we have done,
And now we realise, you are the precious one.
Thank you for loving us and making us so special,
Lord, to me you're like gold.

God must have been really pleased with Jenny – why don't you have a go at writing a psalm too?!

Where are you going?

15 Nov

Have you ever used a map or satnav to help you find where you're going? But how do you find the way to where your life is going?

Read John 14:1–6.

Jesus was explaining to his friends about his death. He told them that he was going to prepare a place for them with God, but they didn't understand what he was meaning.

They couldn't use a map to find the way to God. But Jesus could help them. What did he say?

"I am the_ _ _, the _ _ _ _ _ and the _ _ _ _."

Thank you, Jesus, that you are the way. Help me to trust you and follow you.

Like Father, like Son

16 Nov

Has anyone ever said, "Oh, you're just like your mum!" or "You take after your uncle!"? Sometimes this is called having the 'family likeness'.

Here is a mother with her three children. How is each child like the mother?

Read John 14:7–10.

Jesus, God's Son, shows us what God is like. If you wanted to text this message to someone on a mobile phone, you could say:

c jc
c god

Have a look at verse 10 to find something else that you could tell them about God the Father. Can you write it as a text message?

Dear Father God, as I read the Bible, please help me to learn more about Jesus and get to know you better. Amen.

Awesome!

17 Nov

Jesus' disciples often found it hard to believe some of the things Jesus said to them. What amazing things did he say in these verses?

Read John 14:11–14.

Read verse 12 again. Can you put it in your own words? Does it make you think, "That can't be right"?

It doesn't mean that people who believe in Jesus are greater than him, but it does mean that they have God the Holy Spirit at work in them.

That's how the good news about Jesus, the Son, has spread much further than it did when Jesus lived on earth.

How many countries in the world have you or members of your family been to?

Thank God that in all those countries there will be people who follow Jesus.

Help!

18 Nov

Let me help you

Have you ever said that to anyone? If so, when?

Has anyone ever said that to you? If so, when?

Read John 14:15–17.

Jesus knew his disciples would need help to obey his commandments.

What does Jesus say he will do? Use Codebreaker 4 on page 96 to find out.

☆ ✱☆✬✬ ✡✳☆ ✳★✥
✦✡✳★✥✼

What does Jesus say God the Father will do?

★✥ ✱☆✬✬ ✧☆✶✥ ✹✮✴
✡❀✮✳★✥✼ ★✥✬✰✥✼

What does Jesus say about the helper/the Holy Spirit?

❉★✥ ✱☆✬✬ ✳✶✡✹
✶☆✳★ ✹✮✴ ✦✮✼
✥✷✥✼! ★✥ ✱☆✬✬
✼✥✷✥✡✬ ✳★✥ ✳✼✴✳★
✡✢✮✴✳ ✧✮♣!

Bad news, good news

19 Nov

This week we've read some amazing things that Jesus said, but what was about to happen to him? It was bad news. **Read John 19:16–18** Now for the good news!

Read John 14:18–21.

Although Jesus was going to be taken away and killed, he promised his disciples that he would come back to them. How did that happen?

Read the Bible spiral.

God raised the Lord from death

Check your answer with 1 Corinthians 6:14.

Make your two pointing fingers into a cross shape. As you look at them, think about Jesus' death on the cross. Put your two pointing fingers and two thumbs together to make a big hole, like the hole in the grave when Jesus was raised from death.

Then pray this prayer: Dear Father God, thank you that Jesus came alive and is alive for ever.

Lots of questions

20 Nov

We're going to be asking Who?, What?, Why? and How? today.

Be ready to get your brain working hard!

Read John 14:22–26.

Then answer the questions by joining them to the right answers. Fill in what you might do in each situation.

Question	**Answer**
Who is speaking in verse 23?	The Holy Spirit will help them – if they ask him!
What does he tell his disciples to do?	Because they love him and want to please him.
Why should they do that?	Obey his teaching by doing what he wants.
How does verse 23 say they can do that?	Jesus.

Dear God, may the Holy Spirit help me to please you and to do what Jesus wants.

I give you my peace

21 Nov

Have you ever been worried about something that was about to happen soon? Jesus' disciples were worried that he was about to leave them.

Read John 14:27–31.

What did Jesus tell his friends?

"Don't be RORWDIE or FARDIA"

Why not?

"I EVIG OYU YM EPAEC"

Jesus' peace isn't just the opposite of war and anger. It's about knowing that, whatever happens, we can never be parted from him.

Use the word PEACE to write a prayer. It could start like this:

Please give me your peace, Lord,

Especially when...

A

C

E

Twin trouble

22 Nov

Do you know any twins? Twins can be alike, but sometimes they are very different, like the twins in this week's story.

Read Genesis 25:19–28.

Let's get some names sorted out here. Can you join the right name to the right person?

Rebecca Esau Isaac Jacob

Last week we saw how God was going to send his Spirit to everyone after Jesus had returned to heaven. Now it's back to the beginning to see how God's plan for his people was starting to work out through Abraham's son, Isaac, and his family.

Thank you, God, that you use ordinary men, women and children as part of your plan for your people. Amen.

Isaac's farewell

23 Nov

This is the last Will and Testament of __________

Before someone dies, they usually write down what they want to happen to their belongings. It's called a "Will". In Bible times it was usually spoken by the person before they died, rather than being written down, and it was called a "blessing".

Read Genesis 27:1–4.

What was Isaac like by now?

O_ _ and nearly b_ _ _ _ .

The "blessing" was always given to the oldest son – the firstborn. Who was Isaac's elder son?

Who was the younger son? These two brothers did not get on well together!

We'll find out what happens tomorrow... Do you know any brothers and sisters who do not get on well together? Ask God to help them to be kind to each other.

Rebecca's plan

24 Nov

Jacob was Rebecca's favourite son (check back to Genesis 25:28), so she wanted Isaac to bless him rather than Esau.

Read Genesis 27:5–13.

What did Rebecca tell Jacob to do?

Get two young g _ _ _ _ , I will make some f _ _ _ your father l _ _ _ _. You can take it to h _ _ .He will give you his b _ _ _ _ _ _ _.

Should Rebecca have done this?

Lord God, when we do things we shouldn't do, please forgive us. Amen.

Isaac is tricked

25 Nov

Usually we play jokes on people for fun, but this was far more serious. Jacob tricked his father into giving him something that belonged to his brother Esau.

Read Genesis 27:14–23.

What did Rebecca do to make Jacob feel like Esau? Draw it here and make Jacob's arms look like Esau's!

What did Jacob do when Isaac asked him if he was Esau?

- ☐ He didn't answer the question.
- ☐ He told the truth.
- ☐ He made a joke of it.
- ☐ He told a lie.

Jacob deliberately deceived his father and cheated his brother. Think over the last few days. Have you lied to anyone?

Say sorry to God for any lies you have told, and ask him to help you to be truthful.

Esau is angry

26 Nov

Neither Isaac nor Esau realised what Jacob had done until it was too late.

Read Genesis 27:30–37.

Can you imagine how Esau felt in verses 34 and 35? Can you imagine his anger in verse 36?

When things go wrong, and other people treat you badly, how do you feel?

What does God want us to do if that happens?

Check out **Ephesians 4:32**.

Draw or write in the box about a situation where someone has hurt you in some way.

Talk to God about it and ask him to help you to forgive that person. Then cross out what you have written or drawn as a sign that it is over.

Jacob in danger

27 Nov

When we sin, there are consequences – that means that other things happen as a result of what we do wrong.

Read Genesis 27:41–45.

Look back over the last few days of Snapshots and tick the things that happened as a result of Jacob's actions:

- ☐ Esau didn't mind about losing his father's blessing.
- ☐ Esau was very angry and upset.
- ☐ Isaac gave Esau a blessing as well.
- ☐ Isaac was sad.
- ☐ Jacob's life was in danger.
- ☐ Rebecca had to send Jacob away.
- ☐ Jacob and Esau remained friends.

Please, God, help me to remember that the things I do have consequences. Please help me to treat other people in a way that will help them, not harm them. Amen.

Wordsearch

28 Nov

Can you find these words in the wordsearch grid? Can you remember where they appear in Snapshots too?

Amos, Isaac, Zechariah, Elizabeth, manna, Baptist, Jacob, Esau, angel, shepherds, stable, Bethlehem.

Z	C	D	F	M	G	B	H	S
E	L	I	Z	A	B	E	T	H
C	L	E	G	N	A	T	C	E
H	J	B	K	N	P	H	A	P
A	L	J	A	A	T	L	A	H
R	M	A	U	T	I	E	S	E
I	N	C	A	O	S	H	I	R
A	M	O	S	P	T	E	Q	D
H	R	B	E	U	V	M	W	S

Jacob on the run

29 Nov

In Jacob's time, God sometimes spoke to people in dreams. What dream did Jacob have?

Read Genesis 28:10–15.

Can you spot four things wrong with this picture? (Answers on page 192.)

Jacob had a very special dream. What did God promise? Complete this speech bubble:

I will ________________ .
I will ________________ .
I won't________________ .

Take the second thing that God promised Jacob. In many places in the Bible God makes that promise to people – and that includes you.

Think of where you are going this week and thank God that he'll be there.

Jacob's promise

30 Nov

Sometimes, like Jacob, we need to remember that God is with us.

Read Genesis 28:16–22.

What did Jacob promise God? (Unjumble the words.)

God be my you will (verse 21).

____

tenth I you me will you a of give give everything (verse 22).

____

____

What has God given to you that you could give back to him?

Tick the things that apply to you:

- [ ] Time
- [ ] Good at art, music or sport
- [ ] Being friendly
- [ ] Helping other people
- [ ] Money
- [ ] Other

Dear God, please help me to remember that you are with me and help me to be able to say "The Lord is here!" whatever I am doing.

You are my God!

1 Dec

If we say to God, "You are my God", he helps us to sort out things that are wrong in our lives. That's what happened with Jacob some years later. It was time to sort out the quarrel he had with Esau. He was returning to the land as God had promised!

Read Genesis 32:1–6.

What did Jacob own by this time? Circle the right things:

horses donkeys rabbits
sheep goats fish
cattle slaves

How many men did Esau bring with him to meet Jacob?

Would that make you afraid if you were Jacob?

Are you worried or afraid about anything?

What did Jacob need to remember? (Clue – look at today's title.)

Ask God to help you remember that, too, when you feel worried.

Don't panic!

2 Dec

There's a saying: "Why pray when you can worry?" It's written the wrong way round so that it will make people think. What should it say?

Read Genesis 32:7–12.

Now cross out the wrong words:

Jacob was frightened/happy and relaxed/worried.

He did nothing/made some plans.

He divided everyone into three/two groups.

He prayed/had a meal.

He told God he'd had enough/asked God to help him.

What should we remember if we are worried or frightened?

Plan and **P**ray

A special meeting

3 Dec

Some parts of the Bible are difficult to explain. Today's verses are like that.

Read Genesis 32:22–30.

What we can understand from these verses is that Jacob had a special meeting with God.

What did God change Jacob's name to?

____

How would Jacob always remember he had met God?

____

A lot of things would happen to the Israelites before they settled in their own country, but after a long time it happened as God had promised.

Ask an adult you trust who loves Jesus if they can remember a time when they met God in a special way. What helps them remember?

God answers prayer!

4 Dec

Are you sometimes nervous about meeting people? Jacob was, even though it was his twin brother he was going to meet!

Read Genesis 33:1–10.

Look back to Jacob's prayer in **Genesis 32:11–12**.

Did God answer Jacob's prayer? **Y/N**

Now read verse 10 again.

Was everything OK between the twins? **Y/N**

God knows what we need and he always answers our prayers in the best possible way.

Look back over the story of Jacob in the last two weeks of **Snapshots**. What are your favourite bits? Imagine telling the rest of your Sunday group about the best bit. What would you say?

Then thank God that he was working out his plan through Jacob.

A new king

5 Dec

Ahaz, Judah's king, had died. He had turned the people away from God. What sort of king would his son be?

Read 2 Chronicles 29:1–2.

Remove all the king-like words to find out the name of the new king.

CROWNHETHRONEZKINGDOMEKPOWERIAQUEENH

_ _ _ _ _ _ _ _ _

Do you think he was going to be a good king? Why? Hezekiah followed the example of his ancestor, King David.

Can you think of people in your family who have set you an example? Thank God for them.

Unlocking the doors

6 Dec

Centuries before Hezekiah, the people made a promise to obey God forever, but things had gone very wrong. What would Hezekiah do?

Read 2 Chronicles 29:3–7.

Find two things the ancestors had done in the temple (verse 7).

1 ____________ 2____________

Find two things Hezekiah asked the Levites to do (verse 5).

1 __________2 ______________

Hezekiah's father had chosen to ignore God.

Number the keys in the right order to find out what Hezekiah was trying to do:

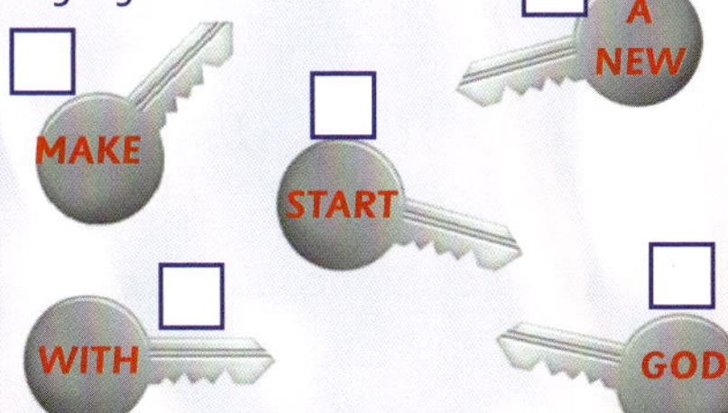

Think quietly about any times when you have chosen to turn away from God. Do you want to make a new start? Tell God about it.

All together

7 Dec

What's your favourite piece of music? What would it be like if some of the band members or instruments were missing?

Read 2 Chronicles 29:27–31.

After two weeks the temple was ready to be used again. Everyone gathered: the king, the officials, the Levites and the ordinary people.

Cross out the Xs and Zs to discover the special thing that they were doing.

TXHZAXNZKXIZNXG
GZOXD TZOXGZEXTZHXEZR

____

____

Hezekiah knew that the worship would be better if the people were together.

Try and picture all the different people who go to your church. What would the worship be like if some of the people were missing?

Thank you, God, for all the people in my church. Help us to worship you together.

Destroying idols

8 Dec

‘I enjoyed the worship today’

I wish she didn’t wear such odd clothes

I loved that second song

I must go and say sorry to Sue this week

Colour the picture of the person who is trying to live God’s way.

Read 2 Chronicles 31:1.

Now that the people had returned to God they made sure that they weren’t tempted to turn away again. They didn’t just sing to God, they behaved differently, too. What did they do?

Can you remember what you learnt in your church or Sunday group last week? Has it changed the way you have behaved this week?

Dear God, I love you. Help me to stay close to you every day.

Giving to God

9 Dec

Imagine you’ve just been given some money. Put a circle round what you might do with it:

buy sweets buy clothes
buy a CD give to charity
buy presents save it
something else ______________

Read 2 Chronicles 31:4–11.

The priests and Levites were so busy serving God in the temple that they couldn’t grow food or do any paid work.

What did Hezekiah ask the people to do?

____

____

Unscramble the letters to find out what the people brought:

NIGRA	NEWI	YENOH
VIOLE LIO	PROCS	KCLOFS

How much did the people give to God?______________________

Do you think the people were happy to give? Why or why not? Ask God to help you to be generous with what you have so that you can help others.

Cool in a crisis

10 Dec

Think of a time when life's been going well and then something has happened to spoil it... an argument with your best friend, getting into trouble at school, a sad event. What did you do?

Read 2 Chronicles 32:1–5.

How did Hezekiah react when he heard that an enemy was invading? Cross out the wrong answer:

panicked and ran away

thought and acted carefully

Finish the picture to show what Hezekiah did.

Dear God, please help me to keep calm and think straight when things go wrong, instead of getting in a panic.

Be brave

11 Dec

Think of something hard you've had to do. Did anyone help you? How?

Read 2 Chronicles 32:6–8.

Hezekiah didn't leave his soldiers to fight – he wanted to help them. Use Codebreaker 4 on page 96 to find the important message Hezekiah gave them.

____

____

____

How did Hezekiah's message help the soldiers?

How can you encourage your friends to trust God?

Talk to God about any hard things you have to do this week. Ask for his help.

Who's the greatest?

12 Dec

What do you go to church for?

You don't believe in God, do you?

Who needs God? I can manage on my own.

Has anyone ever said anything like that to you? What would you answer?

What did King Sennacherib of Assyria, the enemy of God's people, say about God?

Read 2 Chronicles 32:9–15.

King Sennacherib was so powerful that he thought he didn't need God. In fact, he was so proud that he thought he was greater than God.

Imagine you're talking to King Sennacherib. What would you say to him?

What do you think about God? Tell him.

God is the greatest

13 Dec

Have you ever heard the expression "Pride goes before a fall"? What do you think it means?

Read 2 Chronicles 32:16–23

Hezekiah and the prophet Isaiah may have been frightened by what King Sennacherib said, but what did they do? (verse 20) What amazing thing did God then do?

Imagine you work for the Judah Chronicle. Write a report for the front page.

THE JUDAH CHRONICLE

ASSYRIAN ARMY DEAD!

Even the most powerful army on earth is not as powerful as God. Thank you that you hear my prayers for help.

Thank you that you rescue me when I'm in trouble.

A great success

14 Dec

Read 2 Chronicles 32:32–33.

Use these verses and those from 5 December to fill in the Hezekiah Factfile.

FACTFILE

NAME: ____________________

FATHER'S NAME:

____

MOTHER'S NAME:

____

AGE WHEN HE BECAME KING:

______

RULED FOR ________ YEARS

WHO BECAME KING AFTER HIM?

____

TWO THINGS HE DID WELL:

____

____

WHAT PEOPLE THOUGHT OF HIM:

____

____

Pray for the leaders of your country to listen to God and go his way.

Praying honestly

15 Dec

Even though Hezekiah was a good and faithful king, life didn't always go well for him.

Read Isaiah 38:1–8.

Hezekiah was shocked when he was told he was going to die. What did he do?

He p______ and he c__________.

Hezekiah told God exactly how he felt. After Hezekiah was well, he prayed again. He was still being honest with God. You can read his prayer in **Isaiah 38:9–17**.

Now it's your turn. Use the questions below to help you pray.

What I really want to thank God for... ____________________

What I'm angry about...

____

What is worrying me at the moment...

____

What I'm excited about...

____

What I'm sad about...

____

Amazing news!

16 Dec

When a baby is on the way, we might hear the news on the phone, by letter or email. But when Mary was pregnant with Jesus, God sent an angel to tell her!

Read Luke 1:26–31.

Which other person did Gabriel visit with baby news? (Clue – look at Luke 1:11–12.)

Can you circle 'T' for true or 'F' for false beside these statements?

Mary was an old woman. T/F

Mary was a young woman. T/F

Mary lived in a big city. T/F

God chose her to be Jesus' mother. T/F

Lots of angels came to give Mary the news. T/F

(Answers on page 192.)

Thank God that he wanted to send Jesus to earth.

Wow!

17 Dec

Sue Clutterham, who writes for Snapshots, says, "When I hear about something amazing, I say, 'Wow!' What's your favourite expression?" Write it in the speech bubble:

Read Luke 1:32–33.

The angel told Mary some amazing things about her baby.

He will be _ _ _ _ _ . He will be called the _ . God will make him a _ _ _ _ .

Mary didn't say, "Wow!" Read Luke 1:38 to find out what she did say.

If you really mean it, use the first five words that Mary said in Luke 1:38 as your own prayer.

Mary's song

18 Dec

What do you do when you are excited?

shout, clap, laugh, dance, sing

Find out what Mary did when she was excited.

Read Luke 1:46–50.

Who was Mary praising? (verse 46) ____________________

____

Why was she happy? (verse 49)

____

____

Go to a place where it doesn't matter if you make a noise! Shout out to God how great you think he is, as loud as you can!

You could shout the words of today's Bible verses.

Most powerful!

19 Dec

Can you think of any people who are powerful? You may have seen them on the television. Mary's song tells us that God is the most powerful of all!

Read Luke 1:51–55.

Join these descriptions of God to the right verse numbers:

51	Lifted up the lowly/ humble
52	Scattered the proud
53	Filled the hungry
54	Showed mercy
55	Kept his promises

Mary's song is like the song that Zechariah sang when John was born. Check it out – read **Luke 1:67–68**, then pray this prayer:

Thank you, God, that you are so powerful. Thank you, God, that you help your people. Thank you, God, for sending Jesus.

God's plan

20 Dec

When your mum was expecting you, she would have planned where you would be born. God had a special plan for Jesus and where he would be born!

Read Luke 2:1–5.

What forced Joseph and Mary to go to Bethlehem?

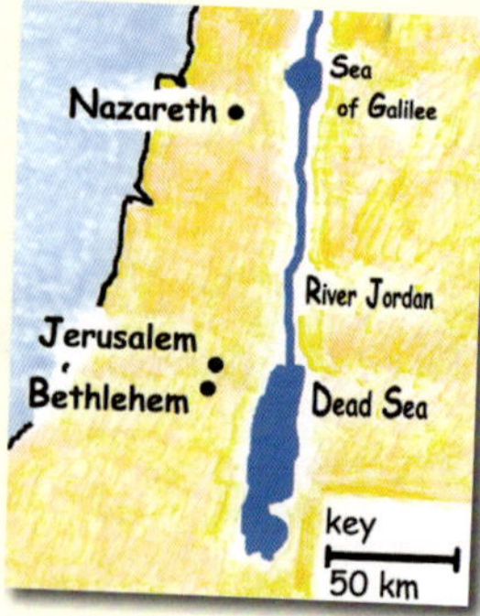

On the map, find Nazareth – the place where Mary and Joseph lived. Draw a line to show their journey to Bethlehem – it was a long way! How many kilometres away from Bethlehem was it?

Check out **Micah 5:2.**

Thank God that it was part of his plan that Jesus would be born in Bethlehem. It wasn't an accident.

God doesn't have accidents!

cot or crib?

21 Dec

Sue Clutterham says, "A new baby sleeps in a cot or a crib. What did you have when you were born? A friend of mine made a drawer from her dressing table into a bed for her baby!"

Read Luke 2:6–7.

After they had registered for the census in Bethlehem, did Mary and Joseph go straight back home to Nazareth? Y/N

Did they find a room to stay in? Y/N

Was the Son of God born in a royal palace? Y/N

Did he have a baby's cot? Y/N

Sing one of your favourite carols to thank God that Jesus was born just like us!

Good news!

22 Dec

In Bible times, shepherds were not always trusted or seen as important. But God gave very special news to shepherds!

Read Luke 2:8–10.

In the word square, find the words that the angel said:

B	J	E	D	S	N
P	E	O	P	L	E
J	O	Y	U	S	W
G	R	E	A	T	S
A	F	R	A	I	D

Don't _ _ _ _ _ _ _ _! I am here with _ _ _ _ _ _ _ _ for you which will bring _ _ _ _ _ _ _ _ to all the _ _ _ _ _ _.

Write down the leftover letters in order: _ _ _ _ _ This is the "good news".

Thank Jesus that he is the good news.

Where?

23 Dec

Have you ever had to ask where to find something? The angels told the shepherds where to find Jesus before they asked!

Read Luke 2:11–12.

How strange it must have been for the shepherds! An angel from God appeared in the middle of the night and frightened them. They heard amazing news, and then they were told to find a baby lying in an animals' feed box!

Pretend you were one of those shepherds. How do you think you would have felt? Write or draw what you might have been thinking.

Thank you, God, that even though the shepherds were very ordinary people the angel told them to go and find Jesus.

Wow!

24 Dec

Have you ever seen or been part of a crowd at a big sporting event who are excited and cheering?

Read Luke 2:13–15.

Imagine that the people in the crowd you thought about just now were all angels, singing praises to God. Circle the words that you think describe what it must have been like:

awesome amazing fantastic
glorious incredible bright
noisy musical loud

Can you think of any others?

Verse 14 is a prayer of praise to God.

Read it aloud twice. Say it softly the first time, and loudly the second time.

If you like music, make up a tune so that you can sing it! If you know the tune from the chorus of "Ding dong merrily on high", sing that!

It's a rap!

25 Dec

Happy Christmas! What do you like best about Christmas? It's great that we can celebrate, eat special food and give each other presents. But sometimes it's easy to forget that Christmas is Jesus' birthday.

Read Luke 2:16–20.

This rap will help you remember the real reason for Christmas. Can you learn it? You can click your fingers while you say it.

From <u>heaven</u> to <u>earth</u> the <u>Sav</u>iour <u>came</u>,
<u>Born</u> in a <u>stable</u>, and <u>Jes</u>us was his <u>name</u>.
<u>Now</u> it is <u>true</u> we can <u>all</u> be God's <u>friends</u>,
Be <u>there</u> with him in <u>heav</u>en in a <u>life</u> that never <u>ends</u>!

Ask Jesus to help you remember him this Christmas.

Another song!

26 Dec

The beginning of the book of Luke is a bit like a poetry book. First, Mary sang a song of praise to God (can you remember when?).

Then Zechariah praised God when John the Baptist was born. Now, someone else has something special to say to God.

Read Luke 2:25–32.

Who gave thanks to God?
Joseph/Simeon/Mary

Who did he give thanks for?
Mary/Joseph/Jesus

What did he say Jesus would be like in verse 32?
(Clue: it shines brightly!)

Answer__________________

God kept his promise to Simeon and he did see Jesus the Messiah. Can you think of another Christmas promise?

Thank God that he keeps his promises.

☐

Meet Anna

27 Dec

There was another old person who had been waiting to see Jesus too. Her name was Anna.

Read Luke 2:36–38.

Are these statements true? Read them carefully, check the Bible verses and tick the ones that are true.

- ☐ Anna was 80 years old.
- ☐ Anna lived in the temple.
- ☐ Sometimes she worshipped God and prayed.
- ☐ She gave thanks to God for Jesus.
- ☐ She told other people about Jesus.

There are several old people in the Christmas story. Thank God for all the old people you know, especially those who have told you about Jesus.

☐

Angels

28 Dec

Angels are messengers from God. They sometimes appear in the Bible when God wants to announce something important. They are heavenly beings created by God and living with God, but we don't know what they look like.

People were usually afraid when they appeared (remember the first words they said to Zechariah and the shepherds!) so they probably weren't small and cute with a halo, wings and a white dress!

Sometimes angels were sent by God to help people in trouble (check out 1 Kings 19:5–7 and Matthew 4:11).

The most famous angel is Gabriel. Can you remember who he came to visit?

Tell everyone

29 Dec

Can you think of any outdoor places where things are advertised? Sometimes adverts are put on big boards or written in flashing lights. How can we "advertise" how good God is?

Read Psalm 96:1–3.

What should we sing to the Lord? (verse 1)

____

What has God done? (verse 2)

____

How often should we 'advertise' (or proclaim or announce) what God has done? (verse 2)

____

Who needs to know? (verse 3)

____

Is there anyone you can tell about God? What will you tell them?

Ask God to help people in your church to tell others about him wherever they may be.

Why worship God?

30 Dec

Have you ever been given an award for something? Do you think you deserved it? If you had to give God an award, what would it be for?

Read Psalm 96:4–9.

Fill in the missing vowels to find out why God deserves to be praised. God is...

GR _ _ T   B _ _ _ T _ F _ L

M _ J _ ST _ C   GL _ R _ _ _ S

M _ GHTY   P _ W _ RF _ L

H _ LY

Knowing all these things about God made the psalm writer tremble. Why do you think that is?

Dear God, when I remember that you are ____________ and ____________, it makes me feel ______________.

Everything praises

31 Dec

It's not just the people on earth who know how great God is!

Read Psalm 96:10–13.

Look at all these created things praising God! Circle the ones mentioned in the psalm.

Why does everything praise God? Look at verse 10 and then write the answer in the crown.

Join with all the rest of creation to praise God in any way you want to. Sing, dance, shout, be still, laugh...

Answers to puzzles

7 January: Gift, lift, life, live, love. Love, lone, lane, sane, save.

11 February: The right order for the chant is: 4 8 5 7 1 3 2 9 6

25 March: Neither Pilate nor the crowd did right.

22 April: Nicodemus knew that Jesus was a teacher sent by God and that he could do miracles.

12 May: All the statements are true!

8 July: F, T, F, T, T, T

15 July: the man's friends had faith; the blind men themselves had faith

18 August: T,F,F,T,T

22 August:

Answer: up, right, right, up, right, up right, up.

22 September: T;F;T; F.

2 October: No; Yes; Yes; No; No; Yes.

12 October: F; T; F

29 November: He's sitting on the stone; he's not asleep; there's a hill instead of a ladder; sheep instead of angels.

16 December: F; T; F; T; F